never say
never

01018059

Also by Alison Tyler

LOS GATOS PUBLIC LIBRARY

LOS GATOS, CALIFORNIA

never say never

TIPS, TRICKS AND EROTIC INSPIRATION FOR LOVERS

ALISON TYLER

foreword by
BARBARA PIZIO

CLEiS
PRESS

Copyright © 2014 by Pretty Things Press.

All rights reserved. Except for brief passages quoted in newspaper, magazine, radio, television, or online reviews, no part of this book may be reproduced in any form or by any means, electronic or mechanical, including photocopying or recording, or by information storage or retrieval system, without permission in writing from the publisher.

Published in the United States by Cleis Press, Inc.,
2246 Sixth Street, Berkeley, California 94710.

Printed in the United States.
Cover design: Scott Idleman/Blink
Cover photograph: Valentin Casarsa/Getty Images
Text design: Frank Wiedemann

First Edition.
10 9 8 7 6 5 4 3 2 1

Trade paper ISBN: 978-1-62778-026-1
E-book ISBN: 978-1-62778-043-8

Library of Congress Cataloging-in-Publication Data is available.

Previous publication information for the stories excerpted in this book may be found on page 237.

Don't wait. The time will never be just right.

—NAPOLEON HILL

CONTENTS

CONTENTS

FOREWORD

Sex is inextricably woven into our everyday lives: from the subtle flirtations that enhance our personal relationships to overt depictions in the media. But despite the ubiquity of the naughty messages clogging the airwaves and hogging our bandwidth, the prevalent current of lust seems to carry a charge of sameness. Such one-dimensional thinking can be unnerving to lovers who long for something different. These people understand more than most that the erotic is a multilayered experience that can't be defined by generalizations. The lucky ones already know what sparks their interest, but novice kinksters could use a helping hand. If you're one of them—or if you've ever experienced a desire for a more varied and fulfilling sex life, but don't know where to start—*Never Say Never* is the book for you.

With more than twenty years of experience writing saucy tales and creating erotic anthologies, Alison Tyler is intimately familiar with the many facets of kink and uses her knowledge to craft a self-help guide that entertains as much as it informs. In *Never Say Never,* Tyler breaks down the elements of some of the most popular ways to play, using sexy snippets to highlight the key points in fetish and BDSM games. By coupling these fictional bits of foreplay with practical advice and erotica from some of the top writers in the field, *Never Say Never* will take you on an eye-opening tour that will no doubt spark your own fantasies.

In my work as the editor of *Penthouse Variations,* I've read countless confessions from the magazine's readers. Whether they're describing their dreams or recounting their latest sensual exploits, the one thing these people have in common is their fearless pursuit of pleasure.

Finding the true object of your lust is the first step toward realizing that mindset, and the sizzling stories in this collection will help you discover exactly what sets your pulse racing. By framing your kinky explorations within positive, fulfilling relationships, like those in the stories in *Never Say Never*, you'll be on the right path to create the sex life of your wildest dreams.

Barbara Pizio
Executive Editor
Penthouse Variations

A LITTLE KINK IN MY COFFEE

Y ou have a choice. You can live the vanilla way characters do on the TV screen. They're clean, oh so clean. They all use the right detergent, the proper deodorant, the number-one mouthwash, hairspray, douche. There's never a stain, never a torn garment, never a mote of dust. You can spend your whole life fitting into this image, this shiny, waxed vision of who society wants you to be.

Or you can have a little fucking fun.

As you may have guessed, I'm of the latter frame of mind. I don't care if I'm wearing shredded Levi's. I don't worry if the slogan on my T-shirt would make the checker at the local grocery store turn fifty shades of pink. I'm a rebel in my own quiet way—but I do have a cause. I am all about kinky sex.

If good girls never ask for bondage, if good boys never want to be pegged, if proper people only get off with the lights out and the sheets tucked, then why bother? When you give yourself permission to turn your back on what you're supposed to want, who you're supposed to love, how you're supposed to act, then you open the door to a whole world of X-rated possibilities.

That's what *Never Say Never* is about: the endless array of possibilities that await when you place a handcuff key on your key ring, when you dig in the closet for four silk ties, when you cue up the camcorder to make a "home movie" you won't be playing for the Mahjong Club. In this guide/erotic collection, I've gathered sixteen stories to set the mood, to spark ideas, to spank your inhibitions—and I've added tawdry tidbits from my own explicit experiences, as well as more than fifty filthy clips from more than forty well-known writers in the erotica industry.

On this journey, think of me as your dirty tour guide—traveling along with you on the road to debauchery and delight. Or perhaps your fetish-clad waitress, in a short skirt, torn fishnets, and kick-ass combat boots, ready to take your order. What are you in the mood for tonight, doll? A spanking? Turn to Sommer Marsden's hot-ass tale, "Beneath the Surface." Got a desire for oral that you simply can't quench? Check out Charlotte Stein's "Allowed" (for fellatio) or Georgia E. Jones's "Savory" (for cunnilingus). Feeling like seeing how the other half lives? Page to Sophia Valenti's "Tangled Up in Blue."

Some of the themes in the stories kiss each other. With tongue. For instance, you'll find a little spanking in Kristina Lloyd's blindfold tale, "Blind Lust," and there's a bit of sensory deprivation in Angell Brooks's exhibitionism piece "Bring Me the Dark." But isn't that the way real-life sex is? You don't slip beneath your silk sheets and only do one thing. "Oh, look. It's Friday. Missionary or bust, baby." No, you move from fellatio to a little doggie-style, then sixty-nining before the anal. Good sex is fluid, lapping and overlapping. Kinky sex simply has more crashing waves.

The stories in this guide-cum-collection may work as foreplay for you. Turning you and your lover on. Setting the stage. Or you might really decide to DIY. Doing it yourself has never been quite so naughty. Just remember: There is no correct method for reading this book. Let your libido light your way.

But first, sit at my station and flip the pages with me. I take my coffee with quite a bit of kink. How about you?

XXX,
Alison Tyler

CHAPTER ONE

WATCH THIS WAY—
VOYEURISM

The audience should feel like voyeurs. Their response is absolutely crucial.

—ALAN RICKMAN

I like to watch.

Oh yes, I do. I live to peek, to spy, to peer. Confession time: I am obsessed with the concept of apartment buildings—simply because I love to think that there is a different story unfolding in every room. And in my world—all the stories are X-rated. My voyeurism fantasies run deeper than solely watching. My number one fetish, as I've said for years, is to know what other people are doing. (In their bedrooms, in their cars, beyond closed doors, behind closed eyes.) And isn't that simply the bonus round of voyeurism? Maybe I'm not seeing the scenarios with my own eyes—but I'm seeing the visions with my imagination. Trust me—that can be even more intense.

As can be expected by a writer in my genre, fetishes I own become part of many of my creations. My characters are always watching, like in this sliver from a story I wrote called "No Good Deed":

She turned her head to watch him over her shoulder, dark bangs fluttering in front of her eyes, so that she saw him through the wisps of her hair.

Or being watched, as in this description from my dark, erotic "Boilermaker":

He felt someone watching him and turned to catch the glance of one of the pallbearers—pale-blue watered-down eyes—recognized the man from warm evenings spent sitting on his father's porch after work.

Or talking about watching someone else, like in a story I wrote for Sommer Marsden's *Coupling 2* called "Reunion":

He told me later that watching Rhonda eat me out had taught him more about going down on a woman than any dirty video he'd ever seen.

In my threeway, spanking, voyeurism story "Want," there's a trade:

"You can stand in the bathroom. Sit on the counter. Press your face to the slit. Whatever you want. You'll be able to eavesdrop on Lia's discipline."

I was instantly wet. I couldn't tell if Vincent knew, but I felt the dampness in my panties. I crossed my legs, and Vincent smiled.

"Of course, there'll be a payment involved."

"What do you mean?" Did he expect me to give him money?

"Tomorrow night, she'll get to hear you."

"Get to hear me what?"

"Get to hear you cry."

I've always had a wet spot for peering into other people's worlds. Maybe this is why I get off on being an editor. I am allowed to run my gaze up and down the bodies of work of my fellow writers. Is there a name for that sort of Peeping Tom, or have I created my own personal paraphilia?

Being a consummate voyeur has helped me identify the top writers in the industry. There are certain authors who know how to spill a scene in a way that makes you feel just a little bit dirty for watching—and when they're writing about watching, expect explosions.

In her current work-in-progress "Bird in the Hand," Helena Black peels open the curtains so you can see:

He leans back in the chair, legs stretched out in front of him, eyes closed, head thrown back. He is beautiful in his nakedness, one hand cupping his balls while the other moves up and down his cock in long, slow strokes. I love watching him and he knows it, knows how badly I want to see him make himself come.

He lifts his hips, pumping hard against his fist, and his breath is coming faster, increasing in rhythm with his thrusts. I can tell he's getting close now and his body starts to tense. He curls his toes against the floor and when the first moan escapes his lips I think I am the one about to come.

Elise Hepner describes the arousal of watching in "At the Time":

She can't keep thinking about fate. Not when things happen with an intended frequency every day that leaves her wet and aching, helpless, as if on cue.

"Thursday at six," she mumbled.

This was the time. She stumbled onto her groaning, rusty deathtrap of a fire escape. Risk was well worth the temptation. She curled her toes, as they conformed against the cool metal grate. Despite the chill, her heat flared. A twirl of her robe between her fingers. Slick silk coursing through her palm. She shifted, enjoying her bare ass beneath the lightweight fabric.

Her thoughts emptied, lips slick with the weight of her tongue.

She lived for one peek.

Anticipation tickled across her flesh in goose bumps that wouldn't rub away as she smoothed her hands up her arms. Her arousal sweetly scented the air. Wet and ready. Prepared for pleasure.

She looked down at her watch.

"Showtime."

Andrea Dale takes the level even higher by adding a camera in "Now You See Her":

Shane was taking picture after picture, glancing up from the camera every so often to just watch the action across the street. Emilie was spanking Katy, and while Katy's hips jerked forward every time Emilie's palm landed, they rolled in pleasure in between the blows. I doubted Katy was even aware she was doing it, and I wished we had a video camera as well.

Now Katy had her hand between her thighs, and I gave up trying to keep the binoculars perfectly steady because I had to do the same thing with my hand.

I jumped when Shane caressed my ass.

"I don't know where to look," he confessed.

I kissed him, tasting myself on him. "Watch our show," I said. "You can see me later."

But when Emilie stalked back into view, a harness around her hips sporting a fiendish dildo, Shane gave up trying to take pictures. He slid down my thong; I kicked it away. As Emilie slid into Katy, Shane slid into me.

I dropped the binoculars. I could still see that Katy's breasts were mashed against the window, that her mouth was open.

We had the lights off, of course, but I didn't care if anybody could see us. All I cared about was the feeling of Shane's thick cock inside me, his hands hard on my hips as he thrust faster and faster.

And Tenille Brown's "Assumption of Privacy" takes you right to the front row:

Joe would dock both their pay if he could make it back to his office, but right now his Johnson was so stiff with envy and delight watching Mack slip his hands down the front of Mildred's jeans that he couldn't move.

So, he stood there instead and watched his employees do what they weren't supposed to do, where they weren't supposed to do it.

From that bump just behind her zipper, Joe could tell that Mack was fingering that hot cunt of Mildred's. She had probably begged for it, too, just a little, just enough to get her through the rest of the day so that when they got home they could really get it on.

Joe ducked in the wing so they wouldn't catch him catching them.

Oh, baby, I know all about Joe. Being a voyeur comes with that little crackle of shame—the shiny sensation of arousal at watching other people's lust. I suppose it's a study in cooperation—look, we're all in this together.

How you incorporate voyeurism into your world is entirely up to you. Begin with a peek at your partner. Invest in a clear shower curtain and spy while your lover lathers up. Make a watching date, when you can spy into your own bedroom window while your mate masturbates. Ratchet up the challenge as you become more confident. Stage scenarios—talk about your dirty deeds to a friend while your partner listens in at a nearby booth. The possibilities are endless once you begin to scope the scene.

Of course, don't be surprised if you win a few unexpected voyeurs yourself.

Fair warning: if you see a silver-streaked brunette leaning in a little too close at the diner, trying to hear every dirty word you share, that's probably me.

TANTALIZING TIPS

- Make a date with your partner to play the voyeur. Plan to catch your mate in the shower (spying through the door or the curtain). Or—if you live in an amenable location—peek through an actual window. (I recommend doing this from the backyard, to avoid being reported as a *real* Peeping Tom!)

- Film a sexy video of yourself to show to your partner. Screen the movie together, or use the movie as foreplay to set the mood. (Store the film in a safe place to avoid spying yourself on the Internet.)

- Visit a sex club and watch. Soak up every sight, sound, and sigh.

WHEREVER I WANDER

JANINE ASHBLESS

H al!"

My shocked cry brought my husband out of our tiny en suite into our cabin, a towel wrapped about his hips. "What?" he asked.

"Phone home." I didn't look up from our laptop screen. "Phone home now!"

"What's wrong?"

"Stacia—she's…"

He bounced onto the foot of the bed with me, to see what I was seeing. I was aware with some corner of my mind that he'd just emerged from the shower, and that he was still damp and scented with tea-tree body wash. But most of my attention was on the WiFi feed running on my laptop screen.

"Oh…" he said.

Stacia was on the sofa—*my* sofa, strewn with the cushions I'd chosen—with a young man. They were kissing, passionately, and she had her blouse off to reveal a lacy bra and pillowy breasts. His hands were all over her, stroking and caressing, and although the live feed was silent, I had no difficulty hearing her mimed sighs and squeaks of pleasure in my head.

"I went online to check that everything was all right back home," I explained, aware that what I was doing might look a little like spying. "Look what she's doing! Ring her now!"

"Me?"

I cast him a hard glance. His own gaze was glued to the screen. "I can never work out your phone," I complained, but it was an excuse and I knew it.

"And say what?" he asked.

"To stop what she's doing!" Which was, at that moment, pulling the boy's T-shirt off over his head.

"On what grounds? That we may have failed to mention the security cameras we installed to keep an eye on the house?"

"I said *No Parties While We're Away!*"

"That's not a party, hon. That's one guy."

Stacia rubbed her breasts against the boy's bare chest and bit his lip, drawing it out.

"They look like they're partying to me!"

"Well…" My husband shrugged. "We're paying her to be a house sitter—not a nun."

Once more I glanced sharply at him, wrinkling my nose. "They're doing it in *our* living room!"

"So you want to bill her for dry-cleaning the cushions, then?"

That wasn't actually a million miles from the truth, which embarrassed the hell out of me. Goddamn, it's not easy being house-proud. I changed tack. "You think she'd get away with that at home?"

"I don't see why not. She's not a kid anymore."

"Rhona wouldn't let her bring boys home."

"Which," he said reasonably, "is why she's so happy to look after our place for the summer. Come on, Adele. Stop being so uptight; you're not her mother."

On-screen, the two young things tangled tongues and squeezed flesh. My eyes were drawn back to the dance of hands. Stacia had a lush body and the boy's fingers slid over her curves like they were trying to map her.

I thought I'd taught her to treat our property with respect. I'd thought she could be trusted.

"I don't even know who he is!" I tried, my protests still screechy but diminishing in force. I could tell I wasn't winning here. Hal had always been fatalistic about these things, even when our own kids were growing up. And he liked Stacia. She's polite and sunny and reliable. Well, she had been until now. Right at this moment she was wriggling all over her friend, and he was tugging at the belt of her jeans.

"I guess he's that cute boyfriend from university she was talking about. The geologist."

I focused on the young man's face, trying to recall if she'd told us his name. He was certainly cute, with rather pouty lips and floppy blond hair that—I told myself cynically—wouldn't survive past his first real job interview. "It's my house!" I complained. "They shouldn't be doing that in someone else's house!"

"What…like we shouldn't have done it in the Alhambra Palace?" he asked. "Or in that hotel roof-garden? Or in the Jacuzzi last night?"

I was already pink with indignation, but his reminders made me flush deeper. We'd certainly reignited the old spark between us, on this sea cruise. We'd discovered we were still capable not just of full-on passion, but of breaking the social rules. We'd had furtive quickie sex in darkened corners, groped each other under the cover of table-cloths and even made love in public—though up to our shoulders in the waters of the Mediterranean. Set free from familiar surroundings and faces, it had turned out that boring old Adele and Hal were just a little bit naughty.

People will lose all inhibitions if they think they're not being watched.

"That's different…" I said, with no conviction at all. The reminder of our own transgressions had thrown me off-kilter.

"You know, darling," Hal started, but broke off abruptly as something happened on-screen. Stacia slid off her guy's lap and the open fly of his pants was revealed to the camera. Jutting from it like the Leaning Tower of Pisa was his flushed, fully erect cock.

That changed everything.

"Oh my god," squeaked I. Not in shock—more in awe. It was one of the most impressive erections I'd ever seen, on or off a screen. On that slim body it actually looked out of proportion.

"That's…" said Hal.

But before either of us could react coherently, Stacia dropped face-down in the boy's lap and took his swollen cockhead between her lips. We both stared, our eyes wide, as she sucked that monster into her mouth. For a long moment there was absolute silence in our cabin, and I don't think either of us dared to breathe. We'd crossed a line here.

Suddenly the room seemed too hot, my few clothes too tight. My skin felt as if it were melting.

"We shouldn't be watching this!" I said at last, but ruined it by bursting into nervous giggles. I looked to Hal for support, and his gray eyes met mine. "Oh god, what do we do?"

"Have you got the mouse there?" he asked softly.

I handed the wireless device over, relieved to surrender responsibility. But Hal surprised me. He clicked. On-screen, the camera zoomed in—right on that stranger's crotch, and the pillar of his cock, and the hollow of Stacia's cheeks and the bounce of her dark curls as she bobbed up and down on that beautiful, beautiful length. We'd invested in a fairly expensive security system, with a decent zoom and good definition. I could see his skin glisten with the wetness of her mouth.

"Hal…"

"Just checking," he said, in his softest, darkest, I'm-going-to-fuck-you voice. Even as I tried to catch up with his meaning, his next words made the world spin around me: "I was right—she's not as good as you." I jumped slightly, and he added with audible relish, "You'd be able to take something that size all the way. Right down your throat."

Now that's flattery.

He backed it up by laying his hand on my thigh. I'd been in the middle of getting dressed for dinner and was only wearing panties and a silk slip. His hand felt warm on my bare skin. There was something so deliberate about that hand, that touch. It took our inadvertent transgression, and it made it intentional. And oh, the response of my body was undeniable. I felt a hot plume of excitement surge through me and I licked my lips, unable to avoid picturing exactly what he'd described: that huge cock nudging to the back of my mouth, and my throat opening to take it.

"It's just practice," I said. "She'll get better at it."

"Yeah, I guess so. She's quite enthusiastic, don't you think?"

"Uh-huh." She certainly was—licking and slurping away there like it was the first ice-cream cone of summer. Then she hefted his scrotum out from his open pants and soon she was playing with his balls too, tickling and rolling them. I couldn't see her boyfriend's face, but if he wasn't in heaven by now he must be dead from the waist down. I have to say that, judging from the girth and solidity of his cock, he seemed to be appreciating everything.

Hal's hand slid up my inner thigh and pressed against my mons, making me catch my breath.

Then suddenly Stacia's head disappeared out of camera shot, and we were left with the young man's sprawled torso, his open legs and his erect dick, which he grabbed hastily and squeezed in compensation for those lost lips. It really was magnificent. It made his hand look small and almost girlish. I sucked my lower lip.

Quickly Hal adjusted the zoom again, pulling out for a wider shot. We saw Stacia push her jeans and panties down to bare a round and ample bottom, then wriggle out of the garment.

"Hal," I said, uncertainly. "We really shouldn't be watching this."

"Probably not," he said, his voice a little hoarse.

"I mean, it's...sort of dirty, isn't it?"

In answer, he took my hand and laid it on the towel draping his lap. Beneath the thick cotton pile, his own member reared a proud head against the weight of my palm. "Dirty?" he asked, wrapping my fingers around that bulge, as Stacia stood up on the sofa. Her ass was as round as a full moon.

"Wrong," I whispered, rubbing my hand over the heave of his erection. I can't resist that impetuous hardness. My own response is Pavlovian. Trying to cover up for the secret seep of moisture into my silks, I added, "Really, really wrong."

Shifting around to face me, Hal pushed his fingers between my thighs and, through the thin material of my lingerie, discovered my secret. "Yes," he growled, pressing the damp cloth into me, then stroking his thumb over the jut of my clit; "Completely inexcusable." His breath was hot on my ear. "You're a very, very naughty girl."

On-screen, Stacia pushed her guy's head back to rest on the sofa-back and straddled him, hooking one knee up on the upholstery over his shoulder.

"Me?" I protested plaintively.

He pressed his face to my hair, his lips soft against the whorls of my ear. "What are they doing?" he murmured. "What are you watching now?"

"She's…um… She's sitting on his face. Oh… She's getting him to lick her."

Still stroking me, Hal turned his head a little so that he could cast one eye on the screen and share my view. At the top of the screen: her bare ass, full and round and smooth. At the bottom of the screen: his cock pointing up like a rocket at her full moon, his hand sliding slowly up and down its thick shaft, priming for liftoff. We both watched as Stacia undulated her hips, settling herself deeper over the young man's mouth, her bumcheeks quivering.

"She seems to know what she's doing," I whispered, pushing aside the flap of towel and taking my husband's erect cock in my own eager grasp. He was as hard today as he had been on our honeymoon, years ago.

"Oh…yes." I'm not sure if Hal was approving Stacia's actions or mine.

"And he seems to be pretty good at…that." I was basing my judgment on the way her bumcheeks were quivering and undulating as his mouth worked at her. We could just make out the bob of his Adam's apple in the shadow under her open thighs. "That's good in a young guy, don't you think?"

"He's…doing okay, I'd say." Hal's voice was gruff. "I mean, he's certainly giving it some effort. Licking that pussy." He pressed his fingers into my yielding flesh as if it were my pussy he was referring to. In fact I could almost imagine that it was the young man's tongue I could feel down there. We were enjoying their bodies visually, across hundreds of miles of ocean—so why not feel their pleasure remotely too? I squeezed and stroked Hal's cock in time with the hand working the on-screen member, imagining it was the hot velvet length of that unknown young man that I had hold of.

13

"She has a beautiful ass." My soft, polite words did justice neither to the voluptuous bottom we were ogling, nor the hot and filthy thrills coursing through my most intimate flesh. I felt as if I were melting onto Hal's hand.

"Uh-huh," was all he managed to say, but I didn't doubt his sincerity.

"And that's a lovely big cock." I didn't know why I felt the need to keep talking, except that it gave me a sense of distance. As long as I kept analyzing what happened on-screen, it felt like I wasn't helpless. "Do you think this is their first time?"

"No."

"I don't either. She's so confident. A cock like that…first time round…Well, I'd be nervous."

"Oh?"

"That I couldn't take it."

Hal had his fingers inside my panties now, gliding through my silky moisture. "You're so wet right now, you could take anything," he growled. "You could take that cock, easily."

The thought made me pant. I watched the boy's hand on one shaft and felt the other shaft in my hand, I welcomed the press of fingers into my yielding hole, and in my head they were all one cock. "Do you think—" I started, then broke off with an "Oh! Don't stop!"

Stacia, abruptly, had unhitched herself from her boyfriend's face and plumped down on his thighs again, hiding his fine equipment from view. All we could see was her back and their arms. They were both reaching off-screen.

"What are they doing?" I asked, bereft.

"Condom," my husband answered.

"Oh." I was mollified. "Good girl."

"Get up, Adele." Hal lifted the laptop from me.

"Huh?"

"Over there. The armchair." He guided me across our cabin to the compact, upholstered chair. Arranging me behind it, he put the open laptop computer on the seat cushion then bent me over the back. I braced my hands as Hal pulled down my panties. Looking down, we could both see the screen.

Stacia and friend had changed position. She was still astride his lap, but now she was facing outward, toward the camera. She wore her bra, though nothing else. Her body still hid most of his, but we could see the dark stripe of her semi-shaven mound, spread wide to engulf the pillar of his cock. As she sank upon it Hal thrust his fingers into my pussy, and I was so wet that my juices ran into his hand as he worked them inside me.

"Oh!" I cried.

Inch by inch Stacia impaled herself upon him. I just was beginning to suspect that her boyfriend was a lazy so-and-so—he hadn't moved from his semi-recumbent slump since I'd first seen him—when he redeemed himself by releasing the bra-catch at Stacia's back and letting her breasts tumble free. He threw the garment aside and grabbed himself big handfuls, pulling her back against him so that her soft torso was stretched taut.

"Oh...yes!" said Hal, withdrawing his fingers and, replacing them with his cock, entering me with a single thrust. All the way. His cock stretched me, filling my body with that familiar, delicious ache. And as Stacia bounced up and down on her boyfriend's lap—her boobs slapping up and down in his cupped hands, her eyes closed in ecstatic concentration—Hal fucked me hard, just the way I like it. Both of us wide-eyed, but just as focused as Stacia. Watching the couple on the screen as they unwittingly gave us our own private sex show.

It felt like we were fucking them: that giant cock, those beautiful bodies. All that youth and passion. Through those illicit glimpses, we owned them.

When Stacia reached down to play with her clit, I followed suit. When she started to cum, heaving and shuddering, I came too. And that set Hal off, so that he emptied himself into me with a groan of relief.

Sweating and gasping, I would have collapsed over the chair-back, except that Hal caught me up and held me tight. "Are you okay, hon?" he whispered.

"Yes. Yes. Oh god…that was…"

Hal interrupted, still trying to catch his breath. "You're such a hot little minx, Adele. That was incredible."

On-screen, the two lovers had stopped moving and lay in a daze. I twisted round to take my own lover's cheek in my hand. I didn't know whether to giggle or cry.

"Oh Hal. Are we bad?"

"Bad? No." His face was flushed, his hair darkened by sweat. He kissed me. "I'd say that that was really, *really* good."

I stroked his face, exasperated. "You know what I mean."

He grinned. "I know we're going to be late for the dinner sitting unless we hurry."

And we'd been invited to the Captain's Table that night. "Oh hell," I protested. "I need a shower now." My filmy lingerie was stuck to my damp skin.

"Yes…I need to rinse off again. Come in the shower with me." The twinkle in his eye suggested there was a possibility we were going to miss the meal altogether. I kissed the tip of his nose.

"You go ahead."

As Hal disappeared back into the bathroom, I grabbed the mouse off the bed and turned to close down the camera feed. Stacia's boyfriend had slipped off his rubber, and was tying a knot in it. It was hard to resent them anymore, but I winced as I saw his hand hover, about to drop it on the coffee table. Then Stacia intercepted; catching a tissue from an open box, she wrapped the used condom securely and stood up to take it away.

My heart leapt with pride.

"Good girl," I said, relieved.

CHAPTER TWO

X IS FOR EXPOSURE—
EXHIBITIONISM

Part of me is a sexual exhibitionist.

—KYLIE MINOGUE

Like salt and pepper, cream and sugar, and *Harold and Maude*, exhibitionism goes hand and hand with voyeurism. I expose myself constantly—in my work, I mean. (Hell, my collection of short stories is actually called *Exposed*.) I give myself away, tear off my clothes, pull aside my lingerie with every stroke of my fingers on my keyboard. Exhibitionism is the mirror image of voyeurism, and even if you think you might be hesitant to be the one on display, give the concept a second thought. You—adored—it doesn't get much better than that.

In my story "Pierced"—it's the excitement from even the teeth of the zipper parting, the knowing what's going to happen:

He turned her sideways, unzipped the skirt, let the fabric fall. Now she was half-naked, and that felt wrong. He understood, pulled the T-shirt up over her head. This was better. Totally naked, with her silver-ringed tits on display, her belly button decorated, her body so pale and pretty.

At the other end of the fetish is stripping where people might see. In "Wrapping it Up in Public," which I wrote nearly two decades ago, the narrator describes her girlfriend's desires:

She needs to be taken in this manner, roughly, in public, exposed. It's the only way she can really get off. She is the truest exhibitionist I've ever met.

What does it take to bring exhibitionism into the bedroom? And isn't that an oxymoron? How do you expose yourself when you're all by yourself? Sharon Wachsler has the answer with "The Trick in the Mirror":

On standing, I caught my reflection in the full-length mirror. The autumn air had wind-swept my hair and put roses in my cheeks. This morning Dana had whispered, "You make my blood run hot," and I'd scoffed. But now...

I let my hand fall to my full breast, caressing myself. Nobody knows what I'm doing in here, I thought. My clit tingled.

Pulling off my sweater and bra, my breasts hanging heavy, I remembered that party trick that used to drive the college boys wild. What had they seen? What would Dana see?

Staring into the glass, I lifted my breast, tonguing my areola, teasing my nipple until it puckered and glistened. I sucked myself deep, thrilling at the combined sensation of watching and feeling my mouth tug at my nipple. Dana is right outside. She could walk in any moment. I flashed hot all over, imagining her on our couch watching me, groaning, reaching between her legs.

I smelled my wetness. I could smear my own juices on my nipple and suck it off—taste myself—while Dana watched. If Dana was here. I buttoned up and hurried outside. With a quick good-bye, I pulled Dana home, murmuring, "Did I ever show you what I learned in college?"

Start with tiny steps, simply reveling in the way you feel when you undress for yourself before moving on to the watchful eyes of your lover.

In "Performance Anxiety," a story I wrote for *Coupling 2*, the main character is nervous, but she works up to the thrill. When you feel safe with only each other as your audience, you can begin to let loose. Really strut. Make the most of every article of clothing that you remove:

I stood and stripped, feeling him watching my every move. Then I slid into the champagne-lace number and tossed my hair back. I was not about to admit this to Josh, but I found myself getting excited.

In *The Trade,* which is a novel in parts I'm currently writing, the characters discuss what it would feel like to be exposed:

Killian had started by circling the topic slowly, "Do you ever think about having sex while people are watching?" He often slipped the vision into my psyche while we were fucking, murmuring dirty things when we were in the shower, or raising the idea while screwing me on the rooftop. Right now, he was thrusting into me from behind, while I supported myself on the windowsill.

"Maybe people are watching," I responded, my eyes shut in case I was telling the truth.

"But to know," he said, breathing against my neck, his cock so hard inside of me. "To know for sure that they were watching, touching themselves, getting off when you reached your limits. Wouldn't that make you come?"

Many authors understand the base excitement of writing about exposure. Liza Bennet says: "This is a scene between my husband and me, and the setting was an exhibitionist/voyeur's delight: a sex party. Our interactions were strictly one on one, but the setting made for perfect opportunities for exhibitionists and voyeurs alike." The piece was originally posted on Liza's blog: alwayseachother.blogspot.com.

I don't have to keep quiet. At first I pant, short breaths, sharp inhales. A sound issues from somewhere deep in my chest. As we climb, as he pushes me higher, I don't stop. He knows I love it, he knows my body has given in completely. If I hold my breath nothing happens. If I roll with it and let out what comes naturally, everything syncs and the roll toward orgasm is unstoppable.

I push into his mouth and hand. I want. Need. Desperation overtakes me. As open as I have become in the moments since we started, I feel the heat bloom in my chest, my groin, my ass. My body is ready to open farther, and in a rare moment of conscious thought I try to let it all go. What I've held tight I now relax. Where I've clenched, I release. And the bloom rises, flows and explodes from my cunt. But the heat doesn't stop, continuing out from the center across my body. I flush all over. I gush on his hand. Involuntarily I clench on his fingers, so hard he can't move them.

He strokes me, calming me. Soothing my swollen pussy. Grazing my goose-bumped skin. He presses to me, warming me with his heat. I feel his cock against my thigh, the crease of my hip. Soon it will be his turn.

I open my eyes and glance to the side. They are watching. They have seen. They have heard. They know now.

J. Sinclaire writes in "The Cornfield":

One road I have traveled could barely be called that. Deep grooves in the earth sown daily by a pickup truck from decades past as it cut its path through the cornfield. The owner of this relic is the one who took me on this road, literally and figuratively.

Passions stirred before we reached the house nestled within the field. He parked the truck abruptly, getting out without bothering to turn off the engine before calmly walking over to open my door. Turning my body to face him, he pushed me down on the seat to dive beneath my dress and between my thighs with his lips. My back arched, my head driven into the hard springs of the seat as I squirmed from his touch. He lapped at me through my panties before finally pulling them aside. The sun beat down on my legs as they rested on his shoulders and I hazily noted the difference in temperature, my nipples hard in the cold, shady interior of the truck.

I opened my eyes to an upside-down world through the driver's side window. Corn fluttered like clouds above a blue-sky sea. To the ebb and flow of corn in the breeze, he thrust inside me and I climaxed around him. The springs in the seat squeaked frantically from the sideways motion they were not designed to absorb as he fucked me. The world did nothing but watch.

In this edited excerpt from "Strong," Xan West's character describes watching a partner climax in front of a crowd:

"Come for me," I said, pulling her hair.

She did, her body contracting, trying to push the baton out, even as I held it there, forcing her to take it. Her eyes were wide and dark.

"The whole room just saw you come, girl. They know your cunt is dripping, aching to be stuffed full. Their eyes are on you, watching. You can't hide now, girl. We can see you. You are naked to us."

She is so strong. I can't imagine seeking this level of exposure, this level of vulnerability. She awes me.

There are so many ways to engage in exhibitionist behavior—from sex parties to open windows, to public transportation. About "Underground Encounter," Tamsin Flowers writes, "It's a short story about a girl who has a sexual encounter with a good-looking boy on the London underground."

The train rattled over the tracks and our hips moved together in unison; but I was oblivious to our location now. Our combined musks filled my nostrils, and I could feel the pressure building up deep within me. His tight grasp round my waist kept me sliding up and down his shaft, each plunge deeper than the last one, each coursing through me with a sharper frisson.

Beneath my buttocks I felt his balls tightening with every thrust; his skin was burning mine and every touch felt like a branding. Deep within me the reaction reached a critical point and an explosion tore through me, shock waves billowing through every muscle and nerve fiber, a trail of searing pleasure ripping my body apart. At the same moment I felt his hot cum firing up into me as his hips spasmed against mine and he arched his back in the seat. A long, low groan was muffled between my breasts, even as my own whimper was drowned out by the noise of the train.

Chart your own journey into the mirrored world of voyeurism/exhibitionism at the pace that feels proper for you. If you're not ready to peel off on a downtown train, sit next to your lover during your next commute and whisper all the filthy ways you'd like to fuck. When you get home, take the fantasy to the bedroom and pretend everyone's watching.

They can see you. Can you feel their eyes?

TANTALIZING TIPS

- Take turns playing the exhibitionist and the voyeur. Who knows which role you'll enjoy the most if you don't give both a chance?

- Describe a fictitious situation to your partner. While making love, pretend that there are people watching. Paint a verbal fantasy using words alone.

- Go out on a date and engage in a steamy PDA.

BRING ME THE DARK

ANGELL BROOKS

Dear Diary,

Well, after fifteen years, Daniel finally got it right.

I don't have to tell you how dreary our sex life has been, which is unusual considering the amount of porn he watches and the amount that I read. But he's never really up for trying anything new. I mean, he talks a good game, mentioning threesomes and the like, but he's never taken any steps to try to make it happen. (How do you go about setting that up anyway?) I thought for sure we were doomed to a life of quickies and rough sex. Yes, rough sex can be a turn-on, but sometimes I'd like to have him take his time, work his way up the ladder instead of just diving in and going for broke.

Foreplay has been nonexistent. A few brief fondles of my breasts before bedtime and a poke-poke in the ass to let me know he's in the mood is pretty much all I get lately. TBH, these days an orgasm isn't even a guarantee unless I'm doing it to myself. And that happens so often I'm thinking of running away with my vibrator collection.

So, imagine my surprise when I got home from work last night and found a gift waiting on the bed for me. It's not my birthday, and Christmas is six months away. But really, there's never a bad time for a gift. Inside a pretty pink box was an exquisite lingerie set. As I held up the delicate bra, a note fluttered to the ground. Picking it up, I read the flowery script: *Wear these tonight under something short, sexy and elegant. Be ready by seven.*

Talk about things that make you go *hmm.* But I was willing to play along. So I went upstairs and drew a nice hot bath. As I sank into the bubbles, I let my imagination wander. Where were we going? To the theater? Or our favorite fancy restaurant? Dancing? I let my hands slide down my wet body, a dull throbbing building up between my legs. I took the razor, lathered up my mound and carefully and thoroughly shaved my pussy. With a gift like that, I knew I was getting lucky. As I shaved my lips, my clit begged for a bit of attention and I allowed myself a few strokes, just to build up my anticipation further. I could have gotten myself off with the showerhead, but I felt that would be cheating Dan out of something he was obviously going through a lot of trouble for.

I did all the things women do to get ready for a hot date. I moisturized every bit of my body, painted my nails—both sets—and then padded in front of my closet, toes in the air, trying to decide what I had that was short, sexy and elegant.

I decided on my red "Audrey Hepburn" dress. It wasn't scandalously short, and definitely not tight, but it was sexy and elegant. The lingerie fit me perfectly, which was a surprise, because Daniel is usually clueless at picking out clothing for me. The satin and lace combination of the bra was comfortable, not itchy, and the satin panties were a dream. I was thinking he must have gotten them at a discount store: they didn't look cheap, but there was a little disc in the crotch of the panties, right about where my clit was. They must have forgotten to take out the antitheft device, and I giggled as I thought about having to go through one of the stores with that still there. It would at least make the search interesting.

After picking out jewelry, using makeup I hadn't worn in ages and sliding into my kitten Mary Janes, I sat at the door, waiting. I nervously tapped my feet, checked my watch a dozen times, and laughed out loud at myself for acting like I was going on a first date.

When the doorbell rang, I just about jumped out of my skin. At the door stood a tall, elegant older gentleman, and there was a limo parked in the drive. "Mrs. Miller, I presume. My name is Stanley. I will be your driver this evening." He helped me on with my wrap, and held my elbow as he led me to the car.

Soft music was playing in the background. Another note was waiting on the seat next to me.

The champagne is chilled, the strawberries fresh. I will see you soon.

"Wow," I muttered to myself. Daniel had better hope he set this all up, because whoever did was definitely getting fucked tonight. I poured myself a glass and settled against the plush interior as I lost myself in the lights of the city flying by. The champagne was going to my head, and I was feeling wonderful.

We stopped in front of a large black building. Stanley helped me out, bowing slightly. "Enjoy your meal, Mrs. Miller." It was so formal, I almost curtsied in return. A door opened at the side of the building, and a woman all in black was standing there with a knowing smile on her face.

"Mrs. Miller? Welcome to Le Chat Noir." My panties got damp. Dining in the dark. The newest trend at the hottest spot in town. She put my hand on her shoulder and led me inside the pitch-black room. I could hear others around us, chewing, talking and giggling softly. Without my sight, it was kind of scary, but very sensual at the same time.

"Stand here for just one moment, please." I felt an absence of presence, if that makes any sense. I realized it was dark, but it felt like everyone was staring at me anyway. I felt very vulnerable. It must have only been a few seconds, but it seemed like I waited forever until a pair of unseen hands grasped my waist and guided me into a chair.

"I hope you don't mind." Daniel's breath was warm on my ear. "I took the liberty of ordering for you." His voice was husky and had my heart doing flip-flops.

"Of course I don't mind. Daniel, this is…"

He cut me off with a kiss. A tender, moist, slow kiss that had my toes curling. A wineglass was pressed into my hand. The full-bodied liquid trickled down my throat, and I felt around for the table. After placing the glass down, making sure it was far enough away from the edge, I reached out, sensing Daniel's body heat. My hand landed high up on his thigh, and he placed it higher, allowing me to feel his hard cock beneath his dress pants.

My pussy twitched. "Thank you for the lovely lingerie. It's very beautiful."

His voice was knowing and evil. "Oh, it's more than beautiful my dear. It's got a dual purpose."

I gasped as my clit began pulsing. So that's what the disc inside was. He had bought me vibrating panties. And obviously, he had the remote.

I almost came right then and there. The pulsing changed to a light steady vibe and then shut off. "Surprise."

I heard the waiter come up behind me. "Please make sure the area in front of you is clear. Scallops for your appetizer." His hand brushed against the side of my breast as he set the plate down. My body tingled in a way that had absolutely nothing to do with the remote control.

I shook a little as I managed to find my fork. I could hear the other diners around us. Knowing what Daniel was up to, I was quite sure that he wasn't the only one making passes at his date. In fact, to my left I heard a distinct moan. It sounded sexual, and my mind sparked at what the cause was.

Until Daniel put a scallop in my mouth. It was so buttery and tender, it was almost better than sex. I tried to feed him, but he removed the fork from my grip. "Knowing you honey, you'll stab me instead of the scallop. Besides," his thumb stroked the tender flesh of my palm, sending a spiral of heat through me. "You're shaking. It takes steady hands to find the food. Now, open up again." This time, he fed me from his mouth, sharing the scallop with me. His tongue pushed it into my mouth and licked a trail around my lips.

I shuddered and chewed slowly and carefully, savoring every bite. My fingers did a nervous walk along the table until they bumped into my wineglass, and I took a deep drink. Placing it back down, I let my hand once again rest in his lap. This time, I was able to find his cock without help, and I stroked it through the material. My mouth watered at the thought of just falling to my knees and taking him down my throat.

It was such a temptation that I almost succumbed to it. As if he could read my mind, he hit the remote, and my whole body jumped into overdrive. I gasped and gripped his pants. He laughed, taking advantage of my open mouth to shove another scallop in. I chewed this one frantically, as the buzzing against my clit got harder, and to me, louder. I wondered if anyone around us could hear it above their own chatter and the clatter of dishes.

The waiter appeared at my elbow. "Would the lady like more wine?" I could hear the grin in his voice. Belatedly I remembered hearing that the wait staff here was blind, and therefore more able to hear and smell things that those of us with sight normally wouldn't.

And I realized that he had probably picked up on the sound of the vibrations against the chair. Worse yet, he could probably smell my arousal over the aroma of the food he was used to.

I blushed hotly, a little embarrassed. As I replied breathlessly "Yes, please," I also realized that I *wanted* him to know. It was an incredible turn-on, to share a secret like that with a complete stranger. The wine being poured sounded like a small waterfall. "I'll just remove the plate now." Once again, his hand brushed against me, this time just barely missing an erect nipple. "Enjoy." His chuckle stayed with me as it faded into the dark.

Daniel's fingers trailed lightly up my arm, caressing my shoulder before moving to play with my hair. "You look gorgeous tonight."

I laughed. "Really? How can you tell?"

His chair moved closer to mine, and he took my face in his hands. "Because you look gorgeous every night." His breath was hot on my neck as he nibbled on my earlobe. His right hand brushed down my chest, pausing briefly to dip his fingers into my bra.

My nipple responded instantly to his touch, pushing hard against his fingertip. I moaned in frustration. "Oh Daniel. God, you're killing me." His head went lower, to my cleavage. He pulled the dress and bra down, flicking at the sensitive bud with his tongue, before taking it in his mouth and sucking gently.

Tears appeared behind my eyelids as I savored the sensation. The air of the restaurant was cool; his mouth was hot. The combination sent shivers through me, even as the trickle between my thighs turned into an ocean. I pulled my skirt up, fully intending on pushing the thong aside and using my fingers inside me. The vibrations were amazing, but they weren't helping fill the need I had.

He pushed his chair away, leaving me sitting there with one breast out and my skirt almost to my waist. "The entree should be here in a minute. I'll be right back." The vibrations stopped as he hit the remote. He tapped his fork against his glass, which summoned the waiter. "Can you please escort me to the men's room?"

"Certainly, sir." The sound of two sets of footsteps walking away from the table allowed me to just breathe for a second and relax. I returned my breast to its proper place, but couldn't ignore the pulsating beat of my aroused cunt. Drawing my chair as close to the table as I could get, I reached under my skirt, and almost gasped with relief as my fingers invaded the moist heat.

I thrust a few times, trying not to push myself over the edge. Flexing around my fingers, I allowed myself a quick fix, withdrawing as I heard him returning. He leaned toward me, sniffing the air.

"Oh Sarah," his voice was low and husky. "You've been a bad girl, haven't you?" I giggled my agreement. "Just for that, you're going to have to wait until dessert for your next surprise." I immediately put on my pouty face, the one always guaranteed to get me what I want, when I realized, once again, that he couldn't see me. So I just sighed as our dinner arrived.

Even without my sight, and my lack of coordination in general, I managed to get through the entree without any major mishaps. What pissed me off was that instead of continuing the sexual dance, like we had during the appetizer, he started *small talk*, asking how my day at work was, and filling me in on his latest project. I managed to answer in even tones, but inside I was FUMING. How dare he get me all worked up, just to drop me in a bucket of cold water?

Well, I'd show him. As soon as dinner was over, I'd take the car and go home to my vibrators—*again*. Who cared how he'd get home? I wasn't going to play his games any longer.

"Are you ready for dessert?" As he cleared the plates, the waiter addressed Daniel. "Absolutely." He replied. I muttered something under my breath, which both men took for agreement.

Daniel's hand reached for mine, which I stubbornly removed from his grip. If he was going to be that way...

My chair was moving! Daniel was pulling me toward him. Stroking my hair, he whispered, "Come here honey. Let me hold you." I pulled away. Hauling me to my feet, he moved my chair. I bumped into someone, barely managing to stay upright. "So sorry." I breathed.

"Quite all right, Miss," our waiter responded. Plates were placed on the table. "Will there be anything else this evening?"

"Yes, can you please take her chair? She'll be sitting with me." Another chuckle from the darkness. I didn't want to sit on Daniel's lap, but there was no way I could safely sit on the floor, and standing was just silly.

"Fine." I stepped in front of him, preparing to sit down. Instead I was pulled facing forward into his lap, straddling him in the chair. I gasped as his fingers pulled the thong aside, just as I had before, but instead of fingering me, he plunged into me with his hard-on.

He was fucking me. I was fucking him, right there. With dozens of people around us. And no one could see. I moaned as he kissed me, this time hard and hungry. His cock was hard as granite and felt like heaven as he guided me, helping me keep my balance as I fucked him as quietly as I could. I sat down hard, feeling his muscles coil as he barely bit back a grunt. His fingers found my clit, stroking it in a set rhythm, and I swallowed another moan. I flexed around him, rocking slowly back and forth. I stood again, keeping the tip of his head just barely inside my walls. I flexed again and swiveled my hips, and then slowly sank down, coming hard around his shaft.

"Honey, I think I'm going to..." he began, and I flexed again, kissing him as I felt him shoot off inside me. My pussy clenched as his fingers flew over my clit in a frenzied dance, and within seconds I was coming again, biting his shoulder to keep from crying out.

We sat like that for a minute, just holding each other. "Sarah, I think we should..."

I moved. "Yeah, I agree. Let's get out of here." He tapped his fork against his glass.

We both stood on shaky legs, as the waiter came over. "I think we're done for the evening," Daniel told him, and the waiter put my hand on his shoulder, caressing it briefly, with Daniel's on mine, and led us out. "I trust you had a good evening?" I could tell he said it with a smirk.

"Yes, we did," I replied with a sweet smile to my voice. "I trust yours was equally as...entertaining." He laughed. "Yes, Miss, yes it was."

As we said our good-byes and walked out into the well-lit lobby, I stopped to allow my eyes to adjust. And appearing in front of me was a bank of monitors. I didn't even think of security cameras!

I held on to the desk, mortified, as Daniel spoke with one of the guards. He was passed a disc and high fives were exchanged.

As he led me outside to the waiting limo, I had to ask. "Who was that?"

"Oh, that was just Kenneth. A guy I used to work with. He gave me a copy of the footage from the camera pointed at our table tonight."

As Stanley helped us into the car I groaned and held my head in my hands. "You mean they *saw* all that?"

Daniel slid over and put his arm around me. "They did. And they said I was the luckiest man in the world." He tilted my chin up and kissed me tenderly. "And they're right."

I leaned into him and grinned, holding up a strawberry. "We missed dessert."

But Diary, we made up for that.

Just ask Stanley.

CHAPTER THREE

SLIPPERY WHEN WET—
CUNNILINGUS

Cunnilingus is next to godliness.

—KALI NICHTA

My hand guides your head down, your probing tongue settling between the juncture of my thighs. I hold you in place as you part my lips with yours, searching for my bud of passion. You find it; I gasp. You quicken; my grip strengthens. You work tirelessly; I come. You're such a good boy.

—J. SINCLAIRE, "PASSION"

Oh god, yes.

I want more. Give me more. Spread me open. Lick me up and down. I devoted one chapter to oral sex in *Never Have the Same Sex Twice*, and you know what? That wasn't enough. And it wasn't really fair. Cunnilingus really deserves its own chapter, or night on the town, or holiday weekend.

I've written about oral delights in more stories than I can lick—I mean, count. Sometimes, my characters talk about what's happened in the past, like in this clip from "Burned":

I'd told him about the time she splayed me on the kitchen floor and licked my pussy for hours without letting me come, a candle in her hand, drip-dripping wax all over my body whenever I got too close to climax.

I've penned that first breath of a tongue on a lover's pussy, like in "Seeing Stars":

We were nine floors up. But we were on top of the world, on top of Los Angeles. His mouth crested over my pussy, not locking on, not licking in. He was teasing me. I was shuddering.

And then I've moved on to the main event, as in "Zachary's Bed":

I moan as he spreads me with his thumbs, parts my nether lips like the petals of a flower. I moan again as his warm mouth opens and he slides his tongue in crazy circles there, where I need him, there, and I can't keep from shifting my hips to the rhythm he sets with his tongue, rocking with him while he laps at me. Laps and licks and kisses me with his magic tongue.

"Zachary—" I am begging, beyond shame, straining at the ties that won't allow me to reach him. I need to touch him, need my hands on his skin, my nails digging down his back, my fingers twisting in his still-wet hair.

"Sh, Risa." I feel the words against my skin rather than hear them, feel the gentle motion of his mouth and tongue echoing inside me.

"Please." I arch as I say it. Desperate.

"Sh, darling," he croons in the lullaby voice that has infiltrated my fantasies. "Sh, Risa," he whispers as I slide on the slippery sheets, pressing hard against his lovely mouth.

Of course, when things really get heated, I like pushing the envelope as far as settings go, like in this gang-bang piece, "Last Call":

Brody pulls my panties down then, and I raise my hips up to help him, but I don't stop stroking those cocks. I feel energized, as if I could do this all night. The low, hungry sighs of the men is payment enough. I am the center, the focus of attention, and I bask in the glow.

Brody dives back between my thighs, and I bend my knees and splay for him, back arching. He's so good. Declan knows how to eat me, knows all the tricks and turns I love best. But there's something unreal about having that magic moustache run over my pussy lips and against my inner thighs.

I enjoy the way writers dance around the topic, making sweet spiraling circles, or loopy figure eights.

Writer Angell Brooks told me, "So many of us are sexually active early on in life. I overheard someone saying to a girlfriend over coffee one day that since she thought oral sex is the most intimate act you can do with someone, you should wait until it's someone you absolutely trust. And I wondered, what if…?" In a "A Taste of Trust," she answers her own question.

I needed to trust before I'd let someone do this to me. And after a year, I trusted Eddie to take care of me.

To be my first.

"Eddie, I need to come, like now," I purred. Horny as hell, I looked into his eyes and whispered the words he'd waited a year to hear. "Eat me."

He knelt on the floor between my legs, his fingers parting my swollen lips. Leaning in close, his tongue slipped out, sliding through my wetness.

The tip of his tongue teased my clit, stroking as he would with his fingers. I whimpered, goose bumps already forming on my exposed flesh. He took his time, sipping, tasting, running patterns through the slick layer of want that covered me. He licked me with a broad stroke of his tongue, covering everything with one rough slide. I shivered. "More."

He fucked me as thoroughly with his tongue as he always did with his fingers, twisting it inside me as if every section of my pussy was a different flavor, and he wanted to taste them all.

His lips fastened around my clit, sucking and tugging on it. "Please. Eddie…" I pleaded. "Make me come."

"As you wish," he whispered with a grin. With a strategic nibble and lick, he pushed me screaming over the edge. My cunt clenched in spasms as I felt him lapping at my come.

As I fell backward, a satisfied giggle escaped my lips. And one single word.

"Again."

In "Mrs. Claus and the Naughty Elf," Andrea Dale won me over from her opening line: "You first." What woman doesn't want to hear that?

"You first," he said.

She felt inner walls flutter and clench at his words. There was nothing like lying back and being worshipped, and if he was offering, she was going to accept it gladly.

He nipped at her hip, scraped his fingers along her inner thigh, and she shivered. Rough but respectful, aware.

But his tongue snaked between her folds, lapping at her juices, and then he moved up to her clit and settled in as if enjoying a feast. She tugged at her own nipples as the heaviness built in her belly, in her cunt.

She tensed, a subtle movement, but he caught it. He picked up the pace, flicking his tongue faster over the hard nub, but at the same time backing off on the pressure, just a little, as she became more sensitive.

The familiar roll started, a wave building, growing, curling…

The wave broke, and she screamed as she drowned in it.

And then, oh god oh god, he didn't stop, and the undertow caught her and tossed her and flung her into another orgasm, sharper and stronger than the first.

In "Ecstasy," by Molly Moore, a woman loses herself in a sultry memory:

I remember his fingers finally pushing deep inside me and the slow firm rubbing of that tender spot high up on my vagina wall. I remember the feel of my warm juices as they leaked from within me and ran down over my thighs and arse. I remember the throb and ache of my clit as he continued his slow deliberate massage of it; I remember the way I spread my legs as wide as I could; I remember the feeling of fullness as he slowly eased more fingers into me; I remember the way the muscles in my lower belly twitched and spasmed as my orgasm started to build deep inside me. For a moment it felt like I was being wound up like a spring, coiled ever tighter and tighter, by his controlled movements when all my body seemed to want was more, deeper, harder, fuller, faster, tighter, stronger and then I remember the dip of his head, the warmth of his breath and finally the searing heat of his mouth on me and then ecstasy.

Cheyenne Blue writes in "A Story About Sarah":

I taste her. I eat her. I push my face up between her legs, so far that my nose is wedged against her mound, my chin wet with her juices. She smells so strong then, and I love it. I lick her delicately, using my tongue all around her pussy, pushing it inside, and then around and around her clit. She's vocal, my Sarah, and she hums and sighs and grunts in pleasure. Sometimes she'll hold my head, trying to direct me, but I've been doing this for so long that I know the moves; I know the paths that she loves the most.

She shivers when she comes, a whole-body sort of shiver that starts at her toes, travels up along her legs, so tautly held, and into her rigid abdomen. She clenches down, as if pushing herself into the blanket, into the red earth, will make her come harder. If my fingers are inside her, I can feel her internal little tremors too, all flickery and shivery. It would be a delicate dance around my fingers, except that she's so strong. She always comes. Once, maybe twice.

Don't relegate oral pleasures to foreplay only. Whether you're spending time between your partner's thighs—or spreading your own legs wide apart, give yourself over to this luscious activity. The rewards are unlimited.

TANTALIZING TIPS

- Learn from an expert. Check out Violet Blue's *The Ultimate Guide to Cunnilingus* for the ins and the outs, the ups and the downs, and the 'round and 'rounds.

- Trace letters, numbers, or sultry designs on your partner, or have your lover bestow this treat on you. The lucky one under the tongue can try to guess the image being created by the tongue-trickery.

- Try a new position for cunnilingus—standing up, on all fours, or bent over a table.

SAVORY

GEORGIA E. JONES

W hen Jasmine walked into the bedroom after work, Nick was sitting on the bed with a pile of her scarves in his lap. "Want to get tied up?" he asked her. He wasn't wearing any clothes.

Jasmine considered him. It was a pastime. He was just the right amount taller than she was, and olive skinned, and burly. He radiated calmness, as if no matter what apocalypse occurred, the center would hold. It had taken her months to figure out that he was as riven with worries as the next person and that sometimes he didn't sleep at night. She felt guilty about that for a while, as for the most part she slept the sleep of the innocents. Eventually she decided what she could offer him was a warm body full of love to lie awake next to and, when he wanted it, she would pry her eyelids open for long enough to fuck him sideways before sliding back into her dreams.

She dropped her bag. "I might," she said. "I just might." It wasn't something he'd asked her before. They had rollicking sex. She loved the sex they had. He'd been with someone else when they met. She hadn't been paying attention until he pitched a fit one afternoon. "This sucks," he said forthrightly. "You never hug me." She stared at him. "I didn't know you minded," she said. After that she hugged him extra to make up for it. She hugged him early and often because it made him happy. Still, it was a while before she noticed his personality. He was quiet compared with some men. There was nothing brash about him. He was soft-spoken, exceedingly polite and his sense of humor was so deadpan she didn't know it existed for a time.

And he didn't strike her as particularly sexy until the day he picked her up. Literally, he strolled up to her and lifted her off her feet and held her in his arms as if she weighed no more than a pound of fluff. When he put her down her knees buckled from uncomplicated desire. "Honest to god," she had sworn to a friend only the week before, "I am a person who always knows instantly one way or the other. If there's attraction, it's always there. If there isn't, no amount of wishing can change it."

Someone was laughing somewhere. It was like a lock that wouldn't open until all the tumblers clicked into place. After that, it was fairly inconceivable that they wouldn't be together. She wanted to crawl all over him. She wanted to rub her face on his skin until she absorbed him. She wanted to open herself up and spread herself all over him. Luckily, he was built for it.

Jasmine had kicked off her heels, unzipped her skirt and peeled down her stockings and gotten rid of her silk blouse and Nick was doing some considering of his own. "Hey, pretty thing," he said, smiling at her. Her belly flip-flopped. She got down to her bra and panties and stopped. Nick stood up, leaving the pile of scarves on the bed. Nicholas Harvey. That was her man. His friends called him Harv, but she wasn't his friend. She was his lover and she called him

Nicholas or Nick or beautiful, though he hated that. "Take those off," he suggested, "and I'll tie you down."

She fluttered her hands in an uncharacteristic gesture. She was not a woman who was shy about taking her clothes off. And with him, she usually couldn't get them off fast enough. "I, ah, don't know if I can do that," she said.

That got her some attention. "Really?" he asked in his husky baritone, curious and interested. Jasmine blushed from her chest up to her face and back down in receding tides of heat, and his cock stood straight up. She loved his cock. It was big, and though it was another thing she felt guilty about, she wanted big. She needed big. She'd been actually terrified before she slept with him that he wouldn't be big enough. He reassured her on that score, as on so many others, generous with room to spare.

He got close to her, placing his fingertips on her breastbone. He lowered his head to kiss her cheek, surprisingly chaste, though she could see the desire in his eyes. "Leave them on, then," he said, as if it was no matter to him. He spread-eagled her on the bed, picking up a scarf.

"That's a Fendi," Jasmine said, watching him tie her right hand. "That's a Pucci," she said, when he went to work on her left. "That's a Gucci," she said, before he tied her ankle.

"Are you making these names up?" he asked her.

"That's...oh," she said. "My mother knitted that scarf."

"Ooookay," he said, untying it while trying not to touch it. "Ixnay on the mom scarf." He pilfered the pile. "This one okay?"

"Ferragamo," she supplied, nodding.

He tied her remaining ankle. He knelt between her legs. "How was your day?" he asked, courteous as always.

Jasmine blinked. Her day had effectively been erased. Nicholas Harvey was between her spread thighs, naked and aroused. What day? "Fine," she said. "Good. How was yours?"

"Tell you later," he said, leaning in to lick her belly button.

Oh, Nick, she thought. *You slay me. You really do.* He had a habit of doing things to her that she was wanting to do to him. Not two days before she'd been at the bus stop watching the clouds scud past, thinking, *I'd like to put my tongue in Nick's belly button.* For no reason. Just because he was hers and she could. He might like it or he might not, but he would let her. Once they had a spat. A tiny little one. He had ruffled the hair the wrong way on a dog's face and she had snagged his chin in her fingers and said, "How would you like it if someone messed with your facial hair?" He didn't miss a beat. He was a lot quicker than he seemed at first glance. He said, "That depends on who's doing it." That meant, if you're doing it, it's okay. So he could tie her up. He could do anything he wanted to her.

He licked down her belly, then up to her bra. He put his hands on her and ran them over her limbs, out to the ends of her fingers and toes and back. His palms were broad and warm, lightly calloused. He hummed to himself from the sheer pleasure of touching her and she thought, *How can I not love you?*

He stretched himself out full length on top of her and it was achingly odd not to be able to wrap her arms and legs around him. He sucked on her earlobes. He bit her neck strongly enough to leave a mark. He slipped his fingers under the lacy elastic of her panties. "Like high school," he murmured. "I'll make you come like this."

She wanted him to kiss her, put his tongue in her mouth, put his cock inside her. "I wasn't doing this in high school," she muttered. He slid down to her breasts, sucking on her nipples through the gauzy fabric of her bra. Now, of course, she wished she had taken it off. He kept going, down to her pussy, and licked her clit through the thin material, making it wet. It wasn't enough. She pushed against his mouth. "Nicholas," she said. "Please."

"How?" he asked innocently. "I'm not untying you until we're done."

"I don't care!" she exclaimed, twitchy and sweating. "Just get them off."

He helped himself to the scissors in the chipped mug on her desk. He snipped her pricey lingerie carefully into pieces, kissing the flesh he exposed. He wouldn't buy her new ones. Just the thought of going into a place that would have them would make him queasy. He would be all in favor of her buying herself new ones, though. He liked her in lingerie.

He licked her nipples, barely pausing for breath. He was more serious now, harder to dissuade from his goal. People made a mistake when they assumed he was easygoing. He was stubborn, with a tough streak. He never babied her, but there was no meanness in him. She relished that. She had a few sharp edges of her own to watch. Put a person like her with someone too soft and it only resulted in hurt. The two of them were a match. They could grind away on each other without fear of inflicting harm.

She was wet, so wet, and her fingers flexed and her wrists turned in the silk bonds. She would have put her own hand between her legs long before now. "Nicholas," she began, but he kissed her, filling her mouth with his tongue, and she kissed him back, making noises deep in her throat because that kiss was everything she could not do with her hands. As soon as he let her speak she said, "No," as if she was the one running things. "I want you to fuck me."

He gave her a sly smile. "No," he said. "I want to eat your pussy." He put his face between her legs, separating her labia with his thumbs and exposing her clit. He liked looking at her. He loved doing this. It was one thing she never felt guilty about. He could eat her for half the night, rest, and want more. Sometimes she sat at her desk when she should have been working, wondering what a woman did without a man like him. He put his tongue into every crevice of her. He loved the way she tasted, the way she smelled. If he couldn't put his mouth on her often enough, he got cranky.

The extraordinary thing about him was that he knew she didn't come the same way every time. Sometimes it was quick little flicks of his tongue that did it. Sometimes the top of her clit was too sensitive and he knew to lick along the sides until she convulsed. And now, oh god, now he was figuring out that broad, flat strokes of his tongue with the same even pressure, over and over again, were going to make her fall to pieces.

She jerked against the scarves, cinching them tighter, all her muscles tensing, arching her up to his mouth. He held her down, his strong hands clenching around her thighs, holding her open to him, licking and licking until she couldn't hold herself back anymore and went over the edge. Nick didn't wait for her to recover. "I'm going to fuck you now," he said, reaching to untie one of the scarves.

"Mmm," she agreed happily. The knot stuck. He reached for the scissors and Jasmine tried to sit up and help at the same time, laughing breathlessly. "No!" she pleaded. "Not the Pucci!"

"Christ, Jasmine." His voice was unsteady. "I'll buy you a new one."

"They don't make them anymore," she said, trying to avoid the scissors. "You can't buy them." He had mercy on the Pucci and switched to the other side, so it was the Fendi that bought the farm. Then there was a brief tussle while she tried to untie the Gucci before he got to it with the scissors. She gave in with a wet kiss to his face; he snipped it in two, pulled her over him and shoved his cock inside her while the last scarf still held one ankle to the bedpost. She gasped as he pushed high inside her, but she felt only pleasure. Whatever it was, with this man it felt right.

She wrapped her arms around him, glad to be tied and glad to be free. He thrust into her again and again, building toward his own orgasm, the hot, sliding friction of their bodies making him pant. Jasmine pushed her face into his neck, licking at his sweat, wanting only to be closer, closer to this man. "How was your day?" she asked him.

"You showed up," he said, voice guttural, so close to coming he could barely speak. "So it was good."

CHAPTER FOUR

OPEN WIDE—
FELLATIO

*A man might forget where he parks or where he lives, but he
never forgets oral sex.*

—BARBARA BUSH

What's that thing people say about men and oral sex? Oh,
yeah. They like it. In fact, one of my friends once asked
a beau his favorite part about a woman going down on him. His
response? "When she puts my cock in her mouth." Simple pleasures,
right?

The act of being oral with a partner is so personal, so divinely
connecting, that whole books have been dedicated to the subject—
The Ultimate Guide to Fellatio by Violet Blue comes to mouth—and
mind. So why not dedicate a night, or a week, or a year, or your whole
life to getting to know what your partner truly craves? I think you can
do better than parting your lips.

Start by simply savoring the concept, as my heroine does in "Connecting":

But thinking of pie made her want to put something sweet in her mouth. And thinking of something sweet, made her think about sucking cock. She looked back at the man. He was dialing again.

In "Last Call," my character knows everything there is to know about her partner's rod:

I keep my eyes closed still, as if I have a blindfold on, because it's still easier that way. I know right away that it's Declan's cock I'm sucking. After more than a decade together, I am well versed in the girth and the ridges that make this cock feel like home to me. I suck him on my back. He lets me work at my own pace. Then I moan—I can't help myself—because there's a mouth between my legs, on my pussy through my panties and my hose.

In "Strokes," Tenille Brown delves into what a man feels like when getting a really good blow job:

Anthony liked when Beverly's hair fell forward and covered her oval face, when he couldn't see her expression and he had to guess what move it was she was going to make next.

Was Beverly going to dive deep with her throat or stay on the shallow end, her tongue running laps around the rim of his thick cock?

Anthony knew he was a lucky guy, standing there over his woman. Beverly loved giving head just as much as Anthony loved receiving it. Anthony could swim all day in her mouth, backstroking in it, treading water...

Beverly had a natural rhythm with her lips and cheeks that fell in sync with him rocking back and forth on his heels because her sucking on him made him unsteady that way...

He liked the swish, swish sound she made like waves, and then... the way...he felt...when he came crashing against her lips...as if...they were...a...shore...

In "I See Him Sleeping," Molly Moore reveals how sexy it is for a woman to suck her own flavor off a lover:

I slide farther down the bed and kneel up beside him, studying his face for a few seconds before I lower my head and take his cock gently between my lips. It is soft and warm in my mouth and I hold it still for a moment, tasting him, and something else too, me I think—he tastes of me from the night before. My tongue flickers and dances around the tip and instantly I can feel him growing hard for me, his cock filling my mouth more and more with every flick of my tongue. I pull back slightly as the head of his cock starts to push against the back of my throat, but then I open wider and take all of him inside my mouth.

He groans, and the sound excites me; I know he is waking, his body coming alive for my mouth, and I reach up and run my hand over his chest, finding one of his nipples, circling the small bud with the tip of my finger. He stretches out beneath my touch, and I glance up to his face; his eyes are still closed, but I know from his breathing that he no longer really sleeps.

This previously unpublished piece called "Honeytrap," by Tamsin Flowers, involves two work colleagues getting down and dirty in the office:

With the lightest of touches, I let my hand run up and down the shaft. Jack's head flops back, eyes shut, and his hips push forward. The muscles deep within me tighten as desire courses through me; my mouth is no longer dry and I can feel sweat breaking out on my upper lip and between my shoulder blades. It seems weird that I am still fully dressed.

And now, finally, I stretch out my tongue to him. A tiny flick across the tip, followed by another and another. A slow march of butterfly kisses, down one side and up the other. I am gently holding the base with one hand, my other hand on his hip to steady myself as I move, oh so slowly, up and down between Jack's well-muscled thighs. With each little kiss I can feel a response in him, a movement in his hips, his back, his gut. His legs brace against the floor, but I've hardly started yet.

I let my tongue wind slowly up and down the length of his shaft, cradling his balls with the softest touch. I pay particular attention to the head, watching as it darkens, feeling a steady pulse in it with my tongue as I circle it, first slowly and then faster. Feeling him buck as I lightly nip the rim of skin that demarks it from the rest of his glorious cock.

And then at last I take it into my mouth, shielding him from my teeth with my lips, just a short way at first, but still enough to elicit a low moan from above. I can taste his precome in my mouth, a little sweet, a little salty, and my guts roil with longing. I literally ache to feel his touch in return. Sucking gently, I draw his cock farther into my mouth, letting my saliva lubricate the trunk and slipping it slowly between my lips, varying the pressure as I pull back, slide forward. I move a little faster and suck a little harder, drawing out right to the end, and then suck ferociously as I pull it back into my mouth. A little deeper each time. My hand at the base of his cock gripping a little tighter, applying a little more pressure...

Fellatio can have an edge, too, as evidenced in this snippet by Julia Moore in "Pinch the Head." A couple up on a convention-center catwalk could be caught at any moment.

There's nothing in this world more exciting to me than meeting a cock for the first time. Each one has a different personality, and Mac's matched his style. Rugged, thick, and finely veined, his prick fit well in my fist as I worked the tip between my lips and into my wet mouth. Mac moaned and gripped the railing for support.

"You're so warm," he whispered, "so warm and soft."

I didn't look down, but I knew about those people on the floor below us, and it made me soak my panties. My skin prickled at the knowledge that my coworkers and competitors were strolling around clueless several hundred feet beneath me. When I stared up at Mac, I saw that he was looking down at them. I could tell that the same thoughts turned him on, too.

Where you choose to spend your time (on your knees, on a catwalk) is entirely up to you. But remember the old adage that works perfectly well for this sort of sport: practice makes perfect.

TANTALIZING TIPS

- Wear mascara when performing a blowjob—or ask your partner to. My extensive research shows that men like to witness messy mascara when looking down at their mate.

- Make a blowjob the main event of an encounter rather than relegating the act to foreplay. See how long you can stretch out an oral onslaught.

- Let your partner suck your fingers while you perform the blowjob to indicate more or less pressure, suction, or sensation.

ALLOWED

CHARLOTTE STEIN

He always says no, no, no. But that just makes it harder for me to think anything but yes, yes, yes. I dream about it at night. I dream about it in the middle of the day. I look at other couples jealously and imagine how easy it is for them. They're probably doing it all the time, in cupboards and on tables and in the middle of Marks and Spencer's.

Though I haven't the faintest clue why I think of cupboards and tables and Marks and Spencer's. I suppose it's just a symptom of this disease I've got, this obsession, this problem that no other woman in the world has. Other women complain in *Marie Claire* about how often their husbands make them do it. They have top tips on how to make it more palatable and less annoying.

But I don't want more palatable and less annoying. I just want it any way I can get it: I just need to suck my husband's cock.

Why does he have to be so weird about it? He's sat across the table from me right now, carefully edging the jam into every corner of his slice of toast. He hates it when he gets a bit that's preserve free, and I can understand why. Who wants a loaf of bread without the butter? Without the best bit, the tastiest bit, the bit that he just won't fucking give me?

Damn him. Damn his eyes. Damn his gorgeous, big blue eyes. And his lower lip, oh his lower lip that I would dance on, if I were the size of a flea and actually capable of dancing. He's lovely, my husband. He's as sexy as sin, and he can fuck for England.

It's just this one thing that he falls down on. This one, tiny, unimportant thing. Though of course the trouble is—it's tiny and unimportant the way a grain of sand is tiny and unimportant, and the longer it sits against my skin the more it itches and bothers me and just won't go away.

I don't know what to do. When I ask him if he'd like me to, he laughs it off and changes the subject, and the next thing I know we're discussing the climate in Brazil. And the old slinky slide down his body doesn't work, either. He's six foot seventy million and built like a block heaved from Stonehenge. All he has to do is hook his hands into my armpits, and I'm suddenly flying through the air.

He could invent a new Olympic sport: wife-hurling. He'd get top marks for always landing me right on the mattress, and for his masterful maneuvering of me into a number of rather illicit positions.

My favorite is the backward pile driver.

But once he's done backwardly pile-driving me, I'm just left with this nagging question: Why is he okay with wild sexual positions that probably don't actually exist, and not with this? Why is it *this*?

I try probing him with subtle questions, late at night when he's half-drunk from some work party and can't seem to get his elbow out of his shirt. He's distracted then, you see. The Crystal Maze of the material hemming him in has all of his attention. I can creep up on him on the sly.

When you were kid, did you ever put your finger in something and nearly have it lopped off? I ask, for obvious reasons. Maybe some rather large codfish scared him one time, and now he's reluctant to put his body parts in anything that might amputate them. I've noticed that he's got this weird thing with his nails. He doesn't like them being touched, and in my head the two things are psychologically linked.

His manicurist was a maniac, maybe. She stuck his fingers inside a massive fish then tried to trim his cock with a pair of nail scissors.

Though mostly what I take from this theory is the sure and certain knowledge that I am going insane. This mystery is driving me insane. It's the only thing I don't know about him, the only thing he doesn't give me. And so, like Bluebeard's wife before me, I'm desperate to open the cupboard door.

I just need a plan. One that's better than the plans I've tried before—which, to be fair, have not been very impressive. But this one I'm thinking of now…I think it is impressive. Or at least, I think it's good enough to get him in some way.

But I have to time it right. I have to be as sly as a fox, as careful and sensuous and slow as running syrup—and I'll be perfectly honest. I'm none of those things. I don't know how to seduce. I'm not sure how to be cool. Usually when we have sex, it's me who goes completely crazy.

But I know enough about him now to at least try to make him that insane. I start with lasagna for dinner, because he *loves* lasagna. And maybe, yes, maybe I persuade him to have a second glass of wine. A second glass won't make him drunk, but it will loosen him up a little. By the time we get to dessert his limbs are all lax and he's smiling in that easy way. He's saying things he wouldn't usually, like *I can see your nipples straining through that dress. Do you have anything on under there, Becca?*

I don't.

And then once we've cleared the table and danced around each other for a bit—you know the sort of dance I mean, where the air kind of crackles between you and every step hints at what's to come—I kiss him in the way he likes the most.

On tiptoe, stretching and straining for his mouth—near climbing him, like the massive mountain he is. And the moment our lips are close enough to brush, that's what I do. I just brush them together. I kiss him with my wine-rich breath...with just the suggestion of my skin, and the slick warmth of my mouth. Like there's a force field between us, an invisible force field.

In fact, that's exactly what he calls it. It was a game we played when we first met, and I wasn't sure if he liked me that way and he wasn't sure if he should just go for it, and one night he said: *There's something between us. You can't see it with the naked eye. It's electric and deadly, and the second we actually connect it will go off. It will kill us both.*

Now, now. Touch me without triggering it.

So I did. I do. I kiss him without kissing him, and once it's had the desired effect—once I can feel him pressing hard and insistent against my belly—I disentangle myself and dart away. I lead him to the bedroom with a trail of my clothes.

Or rather, a trail of my single item of clothing.

Because that's all I've got on. There's just that single puddle of red silk for him to find, before he gets to me—bare and brazen on the bed. It's not a cupboard or a table or the middle of Marks and Spencer's, but judging by his expression, it will do.

Oh, it will do all right.

Typically, I don't like to be so naked. When I get out of the shower he'll sometimes try to tug the towel away from me, just to catch a glimpse of the things I'm too shy to show. He buys me underwear that's hardly there in the hopes that I'll wear it, and spends much of his time trying to tell me how gorgeous my body is.

So I'm going to brave my fears and give him what he wants, in return for the things I crave. It's only fair, after all. Give and take, back and forth—those ideas were practically in our wedding vows. Why not make the most of them here?

"Is it my birthday?" he asks, teasingly. I think he's expecting some punch line, here, some joke that I'm going to spring on him. We're all about having fun and playing games, after all. It's just that I'm craving a different sort of game altogether, right now.

"Yeah, it's your birthday," I tell him. "Come and get your present."

But it's the wrong move. I can see he's wary, now, as he slinks toward the bed. Half of him is trapped by the usual problems, the other half is stuffed full of lasagna and wine and couldn't care less. It's like watching a tiger creeping towards its prey, if the prey in question had claws, and the tiger was a little tipsy.

And I'm enjoying the show immensely.

He gets to the bed and makes a grab for my bare leg, but I'm ready for him. I pull away before he can get halfway up my thigh, which practically guarantees his next move. He kneels on the mattress and aims for something more—maybe a long slow slide over my breast and my side and my hip. It's a tried and tested maneuver, and usually I'd be helpless to resist.

But this time I have to be strong—and I am. I dart away again, so quick he can't keep up. He simply falls into the place I just vacated, instead, and then he's all mine. He doesn't even flinch when I straddle his thighs. And I get no word of disapproval for the kiss I leave on the curve of his throat…or the clothes I remove, as I do.

It's only when I start to work my way farther down that he protests—but I'm prepared for that, too. I know what will succeed, where previously I failed. I just have to make him think that's where I'm going, and then at the last possible second—when he's almost used to the idea, and perhaps on the verge of acquiescing—I bypass his erection altogether.

I kiss right past it, over the heavy, solid shape of his thigh and down to the insides of his knees. He's extra sensitive there, but I don't linger long. I work my way back up, instead, finding all sorts of fun places as I do. He likes feeling the slippery stroke of my tongue on the slant of muscle just above his hip, and a hint of teeth on his sharp little nipples.

There are a million erogenous zones all over his body, and I go for all of them—all of them except one. Oh, that delicious, delectable one, which calls to me each time I curve my way around it. Usually I'd have tried for it a dozen times by now.

But I'm banking on a certain effect, by behaving this way. A certain effect that I know only too well, from a thousand days of being denied it. Force yourself to avoid something, and suddenly it's all you can see—and he sees it, all right.

I can hear the frustration in his voice before he's even said a word. He's now a cacophony of choked cries and desperate murmurs, each one greedier than the last. Any second now and he's going to try to flip me over, to haul me into a position he likes better than the one we're in.

But he's not going to get it, this time—and I think he knows it. The effort he puts into grabbing me is halfhearted. And when I dance away in the middle of his second attempt, then slide completely off the bed…he seems to know he's beaten.

He eyes me with this half-wounded look on his face, but I brace myself against it. I wait, until he's blustery and red-faced and ready to do anything, anything at all. Oh, he'd move heaven and earth to get me back on that bed—and he does.

He lies back down for me, without a word. There's no shrugging me off, or subtle diversions. When it comes to the crunch, he grits his teeth and lets it happen—which seems really unbearable, until I actually do the thing.

I lick him from the base of his beautiful cock, all the way to the tip. And then I glance up, expecting to see him furious and full of discomfort, in a way that I know will make me stop. Because that's the thing, isn't it? I can lay the trap and play this game, and get him to give in for just a second.

But I can't push him to the point where he hates me.

So I guess it's lucky that he doesn't seem to at all.

There's still a tightness in his jaw, of course. And he's balled his hands into fists at his sides. But when I lick a second time, I actually see the strain go out of his body. Those burning eyes turn soft, and warm—as though he never hated the idea of this at all. He was just waiting all this time, for me to break through.

So I do. I lick him again, and again, soft and slow at first but then with more eagerness. I just can't hold back, after a while. He tastes like the salt-sweet of his skin, and then of that familiar and oh-so-exciting thing.

He's so aroused that he's leaking precome, in long, thin trails. And the more I lick…the wetter I make it… The rougher I am…the more he gives me—in every single way. My mouth floods with that taste, and those solid hips of his buck up, seeking more of my heat. In fact, after a second of restrained desire he goes one better than that.

He actually forces himself into my mouth, too rough for me to take. And that hand I can feel in my hair? He's using it to keep me there. As though it was me who hated doing this, all of this time. He was the one who dreamt of it day and night, day and night.

And finally he's getting what he's lusted after, for hours and hours on end.

That hand fists in my hair, nearly painful but not quite. Those hips jerk toward me, over and over and, oh god…the feel of him in my mouth. He's so thick, now, and so swollen—almost as though he's going to come. He's going to just shudder, suddenly, then spurt all over my tongue, and though I know it can't really be the case, the thought is so exciting.

My body curls in on itself, just thinking about it. That usually tepid place between my legs thrums, and thrums, and is completely unprepared when he actually *does* just do it. No hours of patient coaxing, or vigorous bouts of glorious sex to help him let go.

He just goes off like a man on the edge of oblivion, mouth working soundlessly around words he can't express, body flushed from belly to hairline. It's so crazy and so intense—and most of all so sudden—that I'm almost scared. I almost back away and miss the thing I've been longing for.

But it's him who saves me.

He holds me there, with that hand in my hair. He gives me the words I've longed for.

God, please don't stop, he says, the way I usually do, for him. *Please,* he says. *Please suck my cock.*

Who knew sentences as simple as those could mean so much? I feel as though I've run a marathon, or otherwise won some sort of race— which is ridiculous, I know. He even finds it so, when I try to explain some time later. *It wasn't that big a deal, honey,* he tells me. *An old girlfriend once caught me with her teeth—nothing more, nothing less.*

And then I feel silly. I feel silly, for thinking that there was something he wouldn't allow. He's my husband, my wonderfully warm and witty husband. He likes his toast covered in jam and folds the paper in three when he reads it. He doesn't like to drive on Sundays but will always take me out if I really need to go somewhere.

All I have to do is ask.

In everything, always, all I have to do is ask.

CHAPTER FIVE

CLOSE YOUR EYES —
BLINDFOLDS

But the eyes are blind. One must look with the heart.
—ANTOINE DE SAINT-EXUPÉRY

To me, blindfolds are not even part of kinky sex. They're simply sex. Wednesday sex. Sunday afternoon sex. Tuesday in the coffee room sex. How erotic it is to remove one sense. And how easy—with ties, nylons, a sleep mask, a scarf or simply the command, "Don't open your eyes. Don't you dare. Don't even think about peeking."

Oooh, I just got a little wet.

I'm more than a fan—I'm a fanatic. A quick search of my current files shows fifty-five stories featuring blindfolds, like this snippet from my novel *Blue Valentine:*

Next night, in bed, it's me and Justin playing another one of our favorite boudoir games—a guessing game complete with a sumptuous fabric blindfold and an assortment of unusual and unexpected items residing on our bedside table. I'm the one in the dark, this time—literally in the dark beneath the blindfold—and I feel Justin raking different objects over my naked skin. My nerve endings are alive and crackling while my mind is busy trying to place each sensation and make sense of it.

"Come on," Justin says. "Guess."

I feel confused in the most sexy way imaginable.

"I can't," I tell him.

"Try," he insists.

Although I'm settled comfortably on the ruby-red satin sheets in the center of the bed, I am desperately off balance.

I take readers into a little darker place in my novella *Banging Rebecca*:

Sean got the deal first. He understood the implication in my offer, as I knew he would. He was the one to let his lips go up, in that trademark half smirk, half smile to say to Derrick, "Wait here, for a second. Just wait," while he took me to his room and tied me down on the bed and chose his favorite blindfold from the drawer. And he was the one to whisper in my ear, "I don't know what's going to happen, slut. But I believe you're going to get what's coming to you."

Even when my characters are not wearing blindfolds, I occasionally pretend that they are, like in this clip from "Last Call":

Now I sense the men moving around me. Declan tells me to open my mouth, and I do, not surprised at all to find a naked cock at my lips. I keep my eyes closed still, as if I have a blindfold on, because it's still easier that way.

Blindfolds can lend themselves to playfulness, like in a story I wrote for *Bondage on a Budget* called "Your Beautiful Launderette":

Lisa nodded to Janina, and with the grace of a magician, she produced a silk scarf that she used to capture my wrists. Another one, this time in Lisa's hands, was used to blindfold me. Then they went to work. Mouths on my mouth, on my nipples, my ribs, between my legs. Tongues flicking and probing, making circles or spirals, delicious designs. I felt myself tense and release as they continued their probing of my private parts.

Whenever a blindfold turns up in a story I'm reading, I perk up and take notice.

In "Sense of Touch," Tenille Brown wrote: *Abigail's hands were her eyes, since her own were covered in a navy bandana. In darkness asserted by her lover, she lay, arms outstretched like angel wings, legs spread-eagled on the bed. She reached out, feeling for Karina's figure in the dark.*

Between Abigail's legs there was heat that mingled with moisture. Then there was Karina crawling on top of the covers, up between Abigail's thighs. Karina was careful and quiet like a cat.

Abigail writhed, blind and impatient, unable to keep still until…

…she felt the light brush of a feather on her pert nipples.

It traveled down her torso…

…flirted with her thighs…

…and finally teased her center.

Was the feather pink? Or black? Was it long? Or short?

Abigail didn't know and she wouldn't, until her lover said so, until Karina removed the bandana and let Abigail see the light of their daytime play.

In Molly Moore's "The Whip," we get a real feel for what darkness is like:

I can hear Him moving around the room, steady deliberate movements as if I am not even there. The darkness of the blindfold leaves me only with my hearing to anticipate what he will do. The sliding of a drawer, wood against wood, tells me he is looking for a toy, but what of me, I am His toy. Lying on the bed, wrists and ankles cuffed and clipped to the four corners, exposed and vulnerable and trembling…with a fearful lust.

The slightest of touches on my back makes me shiver, the lightest of tickles from something I can't identify. A grumbling of frustration escapes my lips. I hate not being able to see, it robs me of my ability to antici-pate. Many times before I have pulled the blindfold from my eyes in sheer desperation to see, which is why I find myself bound like this now, my previous behavior having sealed my fate this time.

Dilo Keith's novelette *Make Mine to Go* effortlessly mixes bondage and blindfolds:

"It's okay, sweetheart." He kissed the back of my neck. "Keep your eyes closed."

I found the soothing strictness odd, yet strangely arousing. Justin was obviously in control, but nothing he did suggested pain, bondage or even the roughness we both craved in many of the scenes. Even so, his manner was erotically commanding.

He wrapped a silk scarf over my eyes and around my head, knotting it by my ear. Long tails flowed over one shoulder and down my back. At his instruction to move my head, the delicate fabric danced across my skin.

Donna George Storey said, "This is my favorite scene from a much-reprinted story, called 'The Blindfold,' and this part's from real life!"

Not long after that you asked me to kneel when you put on the blind-fold. Then you went on to position my body with your hands, telling me to keep my back straight, my shoulders down, my chin up. You told me not to move, not even to smile. You proceeded to caress me, starting at my cheeks just below the edge of the blindfold. You traced my lips with one fingertip, drew ovals on my chin, brushed my neck and collarbone with feathery strokes. I managed to hold myself still until your hands moved to my breasts. That's when you had to remind me of the rules and rearrange my body in the proper position. You even reprimanded me for breathing too quickly. "Slow, baby, nice and slow," you whispered, smoothing the tension from my lips and jaw until I was quiet.

Whether you simply close your eyes—or ask your partner to do the same—or take the luscious leap into using actual accoutrements, consider playing with the concept of darkness. You may be surprised at the beauty of the multicolored erotic fireworks that burst behind shut lids when one of you can't see.

TANTALIZING TIPS

- Start slowly. Simply keep your eyes closed—or request your partner do the same. Graduate to using a tie, scarf, or actual blindfold. Bask in the sensation of being deprived of one sense to heighten the rest.

- Play games. Everything's different in the dark. Try your favorite positions without being able to see what's coming next. (It may be you!)

- Incorporate blindfolds into vanilla sex as well as BDSM.

BLIND LUST

KRISTINA LLOYD

The flyer had been pinned to our kitchen corkboard for weeks: *Wine-tasting for beginners at Greenhalls.*

Neither of us was a beginner at wine. Tasting it, however, was a different matter. So we bought a couple of tickets and would have gone if, a couple of days beforehand, Aidan hadn't remembered he was meant to be meeting an old friend for birthday drinks.

"I'll make it up to you, I promise," he said.

Which is how I ended up kneeling before our oak coffee table wearing an eye mask he'd bought specifically for the occasion, having taken the concept of blind tasting literally. On the table were six empty glasses. When I was blindfolded, Aidan brought the bottles in. I knew we were tasting red but other than that, I was clueless.

I listened as Aidan poured wine into the first glass.

"Do I spit or swallow?" I asked.

"Do I even need to answer?" said Aidan. "Here, hold your hand out."

I complied, fingers fumbling for the cool stem. Raising the glass to my nose, I swirled and sniffed.

"Concentrate," said Aidan.

I took a large sip, sloshed the liquid around my mouth, gargled, sloshed again then swallowed.

"Do I look like a pro?" I asked.

"Completely," said Aidan. "What's it taste of?"

I thought for a while. "Wine."

"Try harder."

"Can I have another sip?"

After my third sip, I decided the wine tasted of horses and bonfires.

"Horses?" exclaimed Aidan.

I shrugged. "That's what I'm getting."

I heard him scribble notes onto his pad. "Price range?" he said. "We have three categories. 'Cheap as chips,' 'mid-range' and 'we can't afford this so you'd better not like it.'"

"Can I have another sip?"

"You're not meant to be getting trashed." He put the glass into my hand again.

I drank and declared the horse wine to be lovely but unaffordable. "You could try for a promotion at work," I suggested. "Next one, please."

"Hang on," said Aidan. "My turn."

"But you know what it is."

"I can still taste it," he said. "Anyway, you can't drink six bottles by yourself on a Tuesday evening."

"Hey, I've had a hard day."

I listened to him drink. After a thoughtful pause he said, "Mmm,

I'd describe this as…a robust, velvety, well-structured red with notes of plums, bramble, earth and leather, and a lingering twist of smoke on the finish."

"Cheat!" I declared. "You're reading from the bottle. But I was right, wasn't I? Horses. Earth and leather is horses. And bonfires is smoke. I reckon I'm a natural. Do I win a prize?"

"You do! You win six bottles of wine to share with a loved one."

We continued tasting although technically speaking, I should call it drinking. Our descriptions became increasingly preposterous and silly, and by the time we got to the fifth variety, I declared my tongue to be confused.

"I'll give you a hint," said Aidan. I heard him stand and move behind me. He lifted my hair then rubbed something hard and rough against the back of my neck.

I giggled nervously, thrown by this change of direction.

"What are you doing?" I asked. "Is that a loofah?"

"Nope." He printed a kiss on my neck then scoured the mystery object over my skin once more, slow and firm. "Guess again."

"Ade, are you horny?" I asked.

"A bit," he said. "I like you in that blindfold."

"I like it too. I don't know what you're doing though. It's weird. Disorientating."

He kept dragging the scratchiness against my neck until it clicked. "Aha, it's that Rioja we sometimes buy! The stuff where the bottle comes wrapped in hessian."

"Top marks!" said Aidan.

Soft footsteps took him back to his wine-pouring position on the opposite side of the coffee table, his jeans giving a tiny creak as he kneeled. Our neighbor's TV was audible, but only just. I'd never heard it before. A silence lengthened between us. I imagined Aidan was reading labels, but then I wondered if he might be watching me.

I swallowed, feeling uncomfortable. "Do something else. Let me guess again."

"Exactly what I was thinking," he said. I heard him stand and go into the kitchen. The cutlery drawer rattled, cupboards were opened. He came back into the room and said, "Stay like that. No peeping, promise?"

"Promise," I said. I remained as still as a statue while he went upstairs. When he returned, his footsteps made my heart beat quicker, and a tingle of anticipation shivered across my skin.

"Now then," he said. His fingers edged down the front of my shirt, deftly undoing buttons. He pushed the cotton and my bra straps over my shoulders then, taking things up a notch, he pushed both my shirt and bra farther down, baring my breasts while lightly trapping my arms by my side. He took care not to touch my flesh. The exposure and my blindness made me feel vulnerable and slutty, as if there were a distance between us that meant we could be strangers, me a poor captive being displayed for his gaze.

"Sorry, I've got another idea," he said. "Hang on."

He darted off again, taking the stairs two at a time, then came thundering back down. I listened, motionless, as he cleared bottles and glasses from the table. This game was starting to develop.

"Okay, hands behind your back, please," he said.

I did as told and he wound fabric around my wrists, tying them together.

"I hope that's not one of my nice scarves," I said.

"It isn't," he replied. "Well, I don't like it."

I laughed, half amusement, half nerves. Bound and blindfolded, I waited, my clothes bunched around my arms, my nipples crinkling as if they'd been touched.

"What's this?" asked Aidan, his voice a murmur. He started at my shoulder and ran a track of pinpricks across my chest to my other shoulder. He did the same across my back, causing my spine to arch as if my body were retreating from the mild pain, even though I liked it. The faint *tick-tick* of a wheel made me guess he was rolling out something across my skin. Pizza cutter? Surely not. Anyway, the sensation was too uneven. I racked my brains for several seconds before it dawned on me it must be our pastry wheel. But I kept quiet, feigning bafflement so he would carry on.

Varying the force, Aidan ran the implement this way and that, tracing curves and lines. When he rolled the wheel toward my breasts, I tensed, fearing pain. His touch became gentler and I groaned quietly as prickles advanced across my heavy flesh.

"Pastry wheel," I said, hearing the catch of lust in my throat.

"Good girl," he said. I didn't know if he was commending me on my answer or on how I'd held still, accepting and trusting, but either way I liked the words. "Now this," he said, setting down one object and picking up another.

I flinched at the new texture then settled into it as Aidan moved soft bristles across my back and above my breasts.

"Hairbrush," I said. "Easy."

"Well done." Aidan pressed the pad of spines to the underswell of one breast, bounced upward, then repeated the action on the other side. Finally, he swept the brush across my nipples, shifting quickly from one breast to the other. The harshness and hint of aggression made me gasp, and my groin pulsed greedily.

I heard him drop the brush on the floor. For a while nothing happened and I waited, my skin sensitized and alert to a touch that might land anywhere, from any angle. The more he drew out the moment, the wetter I became. The silence stretched until I giggled anxiously. I felt adrift, dislocated. I wanted to know what he was doing yet at the same time, the prolonged uncertainty heightened my hunger. I remembered how delicious anticipation could be and realized we didn't have much of that in our sex life these days. We knew each other too well and generally just got on with things.

Eventually, I couldn't bear the silence any longer. "What are you doing?" I asked. No answer. I strained for the sound of his breathing. Nothing. "Where are you?" I asked, feeling a little panicky.

"Over here." His voice, coming from several feet away, startled me. In my mind, he was still kneeling on the other side of the coffee table.

"Ade, what are you doing?"

At length, he said, "Messing with your mind."

"Well, it's working," I replied.

Moments later, I jumped again as something touched my back, abrasive and initially pleasant, like scratching yourself hard when you're itching. Aidan swirled the coarseness over my skin, making me wince when he rubbed an area more than once.

"Shower puff?" I said, although I knew it wasn't. The rasp was crueler.

"Try again," he said, bringing the roughness over my shoulder and down. I was feeling braver now, and I didn't flinch as he rubbed whatever it was over my nipples.

"Jeez, is that sandpaper?" I asked.

"Nope. That's two incorrect guesses. Three incorrect guesses in a row and I spank you."

I laughed. "Now I don't know if I should try harder or play dumb."

"Your call," he said.

"Give me a clue."

"Think kitchen."

"Pan scourer!" I said.

"Correct. Wire wool on your nipples. Is it good?"

"Sort of. I preferred the hairbrush. Something else, please."

73

"Okay, take your knickers off."

I wriggled them down from under my skirt then sat back on my heels.

"Open your legs," said Aidan.

I hitched up my skirt and shuffled my knees wider. Aidan touched me. "You're so wet," he said.

"Uh-huh."

He held me open and squashed a bulky softness there. "How's that?"

"Nice," I replied.

"Hold it there between your pussy lips."

"What is it?"

"Still the pan scourer."

"Oh. Doesn't feel like it." Without the pressure of his hand, the prickliness was absent. Instead, I just had a delicate weight of texture between my thighs, my moist crease enveloping the cool, crisp sponge and leaving me hyperaware of where my arousal was focused.

The next object I guessed immediately from the smell. Chamois leather. Aidan smoothed it over my skin, its suppleness a velvet caress where my skin was slightly tender from the scourer.

"Okay, another," he said, removing the leather cloth. "This is different. You need to keep very still."

I barely breathed as he touched one breast, pinching a fold of skin between his fingers. The squeeze grew harder, and I realized he'd attached something to me. He did the same on my other breast, closer to my nipple this time. The pain, though still mild, went up a notch.

"That okay?" he asked.

"Yes, nice. What is it? A hair clip?"

"One guess gone," he said.

"I don't know. Something from your toolbox. A man thing that I wouldn't know the name of."

"One guess left." He took a nipple between his fingers. "Tell me if this is too much."

Tightness surrounded my nipple, then gripped it. I could no longer feel the earlier two pinches. "Ah! Ow! No, that's fine, it's good."

He tapped the things he'd attached to me, bringing the sensation back. "This next one will be obvious," he said, "so it's not part of the guessing game."

I heard a gentle whirr and immediately recognized the sound as belonging to one of our electric toothbrushes. He traced the smooth side around my breasts, and I knew where he was heading. He rummaged beneath my skirt, pressed the buzzing pad to one inner thigh then to the other. Moving higher, he vibrated it against my pussy lips where the pan scourer was still lodged. My groin throbbed and I ached to feel the touch on my clitoris. He teased a long time, buzzing the toothbrush over my swollen lips and near my clit but never on it.

"Ade, please," I said. "I want to come. I need to."

"What's your third guess?"

"I don't know," I said. "Please let me come."

"Guess," he said.

"You sod," I whispered.

He chuckled, clearly enjoying how he was tormenting me. He flicked the attachments on my breasts and my need spiked.

"What are they?" He touched the toothbrush to my clit for a second or two then withdrew it.

"Damn, I don't know. I can't think straight when you're doing that."

"Do you want me to stop?"

"No."

"Then take a guess," he said.

"I really don't know. Please."

"Do you give up?"

"No," I said. "But I don't know. Maybe. Um, oh god, those clips we have holding up the curtain in the utility room?"

"Well done," he said, moving the toothbrush onto my clit. "They're clothespins. So wrong but well done. Because I really, really want to spank you. I want to bend you over the coffee table and spank you till you're pink."

His words edged me closer as the toothbrush trembled on my clit, vibrating hard where I was engorged and receptive. Its touch was better than my vibrator, more of a fast rocking than a wasp-like buzz. Behind the darkness of my mask, I thought of being powerless beneath Aidan, his hand landing on my bared ass. My orgasm tightened, rose and spilled over. The spasms clutched and I whimpered until I was wrung out, weak from coming.

Aidan didn't let up. Even though I was as floppy as a rag doll, he guided me toward the coffee table, half-lifting me, half-guiding me, until I was laid awkwardly over its surface, my head hanging, my arms still tethered. The scourer fell from between my thighs. Aidan shoved my skirt higher, exposing my buttocks.

"Guess," he said.

A sharp tap cracked onto my ass with the sound of a dull pop. It wasn't his hand. He hit me over and over, the impact of every blow accumulating, making my flesh hotter and more tender. He spanked one buttock then the other, then went back to his first target.

"Wooden spoon," I gasped.

"Yes," he hissed. He hit me harder and faster but it was impossible to say whether this was a reward, a punishment or simply him getting into his stride. But the reason didn't matter because I was getting into it too. Who cares about motivation when you're both flying high?

When my ass was quivering and flushed with heat, Aidan cast the spoon aside.

"Guess," he said, jerking my hips toward him.

I heard him unzip and felt him nudge at my entrance. "You," I said. "Your cock, your cock."

He plunged into me, strong and straight, his hands gripping my blushing ass. "That's right," he said, thrusting in and out. "My cock, my cock."

He fucked me as I lay over the table, unable to touch him, unable to see. My ass was on fire and I felt stuffed full of him, all my sensory awareness centered on his driving cock and the ripples of pleasure radiating out from my core to my tenderized butt. He fretted my clit and I came again. Minutes later so did he, fingers digging into my bruised cheeks as he hollered his bliss.

When he withdrew from me he said, "Guess."

I laughed softly. "Your come."

He untied me, helping me off the table before removing my blindfold. I blinked hard. The room seemed so bright, so packed with furniture, pictures and strewn magazines. We sat against the sofa for a while, catching our breath. Then I picked up the blindfold from the floor, stretched the elastic over Aidan's head and secured the fabric over his eyes.

He gave a tentative laugh.

"Guess," I said.

CHAPTER SIX

TIED AND TEASED—

BEGINNING BONDAGE

A dame that knows the ropes isn't likely to get tied up.

—MAE WEST

*B*ondage is such a loaded word. What do *you* see when you think of bondage? Dungeons? Black leather? Dark, sinister tools and implements? (May I come over to your house tonight? May I bring a friend?) Sometimes people forget that kink can come in a variety of, oh, let's just say it, shades. You don't need to dive into the deep end right away if bondage is something new to you. Play light. Tiptoe into the world of BDSM (in a pair of high-heeled patent-leather boots, of course). Use your imagination before you reach for cuffs, whips, floggers, crops…those can come later. You can come right now.

But how do you even begin?

X-rated, X-rated, read all about it. My number one piece of advice for couples wanting to delve into new territories is to read some smut.

(Which you're doing right now, you good pupil.) Discover what makes you hard, what makes you wet, and decide first of all whether the words are enough. Maybe you can get off simply on hearing about what other people like to do. If not, then go slow. Choose a safeword. Check in constantly. Invest in a safety manual. And have fun. Sex shouldn't be so serious that you can't crack a smile while cracking that whip.

Admittedly, my novice days are long behind me. But that doesn't mean I can't remember the first shivery thrill of being tied down the first time. Bondage can rely simply on a command, like in my short story "Playing for Keeps":

My training began as soon as we'd moved in together, our first night in our new house.

"Let go of the headboard, Sarah, and we'll have a much more humiliating lesson tomorrow," he assured me.

Staying still for a whipping, staying still on my own accord, is nearly impossible for me. Being tied down is so much easier. So much less work. There is no choice involved. No mental trauma. But holding steady, wrists overhead, body clenched, back and thighs and cunt whipped severely. That takes will.

Bondage can happen when you least expect it, like in one of the first stories I ever wrote, "Zachary's Bed":

Zachary's bed is in the middle of his room, and I am in the middle of his bed. My arms are tied above my head to the curlicues of brass that make up the frame. My ankles are fixed to the railing, my legs spread wide apart beneath the thin, satin sheet. The bindings are simply old silk ties of Zachary's, secure, but not constrictive. One of the ties has a painting of a naked lady on it. I look up and meet her eyes before calling out my lover's name.

"Zachary?"

I wasn't bound like this when we went to bed. It truly is amazing what I can sleep through.

Of course, once you grow accustomed to playing with ropes, there are so many ways to extend the pleasure. Like being tied down and shaved in this scene from my story called "Reunion":

"He was a bondage geek. He loved tying girls up. God, I miss college. Everyone seemed to wear their fetish on their sleeve. Do you know what I mean? You could tell when people were discovering something that worked for them."

"I don't know..." I drawled. "There were also a lot of shaving-cream fights, and bringing beer into the dorm in big suitcases and that incident with the Jell-O in the washing machine."

"Sometimes people need a little beer to discover what works for them," Jill said matter-of-factly. "Like after one of those shaving-cream fights, Jason tied me down and shaved my pussy."

"Are you serious?"

"He didn't even tell me what he was going to do. He simply asked if I was okay being bound, and I told him I'd never been before. He took four ties—university ties, I swear—and he bound me down on his bed."

Or being tied down and spanked, like in a short I wrote called "Obsessed":

"After he came to the bedroom, he tied me down to his bed and he used his bare hand on me."

"Only his hand?"

"That night, yeah. Later on, he used his belt. But that first night, he simply gave me a hand spanking."

"And you liked it?"

"I loved it."

"Slut."

Or being tied down, stripped and flogged, like in my story "The Last Goodbye":

He carried me back to the bed, spread me out, and tied me to Janelle's bed frame like the bondage pro he was. He cut my skirt off, cut my T-shirt away, then ran his fingertips over the shaved skin of my pussy. I had only my thigh-high fishnets on now. Nothing to protect me.

"You know you're a bad girl," he said, "don't you?"

I nodded, and then immediately whispered, "Yes, Connor."

"And you know tonight I'm going to make you scream."

Tears started running down my cheeks. I was shivering all over, but I managed to say, "Yes, Connor."

He reached for the suede flogger, and then he looked at me, fiercely, and said, "And you know you need this."

Or even being tied down in a place you shouldn't be, like in Lucia Dixon's "Quiet, Quiet":

Joshua found a rhythm that went dark and velvety in my head, taking me to faraway places with his cock, with the heat that was still in my skin, with the shame that colored my face and made me shut my eyes together even more tightly.

He whispered things to me while he fucked me, told me how pretty I looked captured to the bed. Captured so simply and purely to his mother's bed. The whole fantasy was mixed up, messed up, twisted and dirty, and it made me come, as he must have known it would. Made me come in a series of rapid bucking movements that almost drove him out of me. He held on, though; he's a fighter, kept on going until it was his turn, until he gripped into my arms, bit my shoulder hard through the silky fabric of my dress and hissed, "Dirty girl. Such a dirty girl. Coming in my mother's bed."

Joshua cradled me afterward, brushed my hair out of my eyes, slid the cuffs off and rubbed the skin on my wrists. He kissed my blushing cheeks and my forehead and the tip of my nose and then whispered to me of how long he'd planned it, how much thought had gone into this tryst. How I couldn't have avoided it if I'd wanted to.

Happily, you don't have to follow any specific rules when you try bondage. In "Confession," author Jenny Lyn writes:

Cuffs of thick leather or strips of fragile lace. I honestly do not care. Rough hemp rope or sticky licorice whips. The material is immaterial, sometimes. It's not always about the marks, although I love those too. I don't always need souvenirs. We all know what it's really about: my acquiescence, your control. It's about trust, yours and mine. I won't struggle, not if I'm a good girl. Your long strong fingers wrapped around both my wrists or simply words. Doesn't really matter to me. You could tie me down with overcooked spaghetti noodles and I'd happily obey you.

In "Clingy," Giselle Renarde's characters get creative:

When Jack appeared at her bedside with a box of plastic wrap in hand, Lollie laughed. "What is this? You're going to make me a dress out of cling film?"

He tossed the covers off the bed, exposing everything, right down to the shimmering pink polish he'd put on her toenails last time he was over.

"Not a dress," he said, tearing off a sheet of plastic. He fought with it, trying to get it to stop sticking to itself, but ultimately it was too clingy for its own good. Picking up the box again, he pulled out another sheet. This time he didn't tear it off until he'd wrapped it four times around her ankles. Her bones knocked together, and she tried to shift her feet, but the cling film allowed little give.

She smiled at Jack as he lifted her shoulders up from the bed. With her ankles bound, she had to steady herself with her hands against the mattress. It was odd, though, how he'd cling-wrapped her legs shut. Maybe he planned to flip her over and take her from behind. Her insides tingled with anticipation. "I love being tied up, you know. It makes me feel totally at your mercy."

"That's because you are," he said.

Total mercy. Oh, let's say those words together. Total. Mercy.

Can anything be sexier than that? Why not find out for yourself.

TANTALIZING TIPS

- Bondage begins in the mind. Start with a simple command, such as "Stay." See how that works for you and your partner before moving forward.

- See how creative you can be with household equipment such as scarves, ties, rope, climbing cables, or wallet chains. Do-it-yourself takes on a whole new thrill when referring to sex!

- Visit your favorite sex toy store to explore the wonderful world of bondage toys. From utilitarian steel cuffs to pink leopard-print, there is definitely something for every type of desire.

SILK

TERESA NOELLE ROBERTS

Dan tucked in the ends of the red silk scarf that adorned Jessie's right wrist. "There," Dan said. "Very '80s rocker."

"This one is more '80s yuppie." She brandished her left hand, adorned with a yellow and red paisley scarf-bracelet. The scarf had been a gift from her grandmother, something she never wore, but didn't have the heart to give away. It had been the only other long, thin scarf she could dig up on short notice when Dan had the Idea.

Dan had lots of Ideas. It was one of his charms, along with a roguish smile, intense blue eyes, and the ability to re-create just about anything they ever tried and liked at a restaurant. He had a tight, muscular body, a clever tongue, and a fantastic cock, too, but without all the Ideas, Jessie wouldn't have found the physical attributes nearly as interesting.

This particular Idea was simple in concept.

Jessie would wear the scarves on her wrist while they met friends for dinner.

When they got home, Dan would use those same scarves to tie her wrists to the bed.

Simple, but as it was turning out, devious and devilishly effective.

Jessie was already wet. She'd started getting excited when he'd first told her about the Idea. She'd been twitchy and shifting in her seat so her clit and pussy lips rubbed against each other once they began working out how to make the scarves look like accessories (misguided ones, but fashion wasn't the point), and her nipples rubbed plaintively against her bra as soon as the silk touched her skin. But now she was slick, her little red panties damp and warm.

And they hadn't even gotten out the door yet.

Knowing she'd be tied to the bed for wild weasel sex when they got home would be tantalizing. They'd already proven through several of Dan's previous Ideas that she loved being tied down, and she had an active imagination. But the subtle reminder at her wrists was going to make her crazy long before she got home.

Dan ran his index finger along her jawline and down the sensitive skin on the side of her neck. Jessie shivered. The finger continued its journey, tracing along her collarbone to the hollow of her throat and from there dipping down toward her cleavage.

Dan's touch made the silk on her wrists snugger—dangerous somehow, but in a good way. She couldn't help imagining her wrists bound together over her head and attached to the bed frame as Dan lightly, teasingly, caressed her. Before his finger reached below the V-neck of her shirt, Jessie was breathing raggedly. She arched her back like a cat, seeking more contact.

Dan grinned. "It's already working," he said, his voice smug.

"No, not really." She couldn't help playing with him when he sounded so damn pleased with himself. "That just felt nice. You know my collarbone's sensitive, and it's always sexy when you do the teasing-at-the-neckline thing."

"Right," he said. "Sure." Then, without warning, he cupped his hand between her legs. "Very warm. Warm and a little damp."

She pressed forward into his hand. "Okay, Okay, it's affecting me. I'm already horny and if you keep teasing me like that, I'm going to tackle you right here in the living room and we'll never make it out the door."

He pulled his hand away. "And miss half-price tapas at Alicante? Steve and Mary said the Groupon was expiring, so it's now or never."

She tried one more tactic. "Alicante's good, but you could make better tapas at home."

"If we had the ingredients, and about a week to plan, and a bunch of friends coming over to share them with, maybe. But tonight we're going out." He laughed, and it was the kind of laugh that stroked her clit as precisely as a finger. "And you're going to be thinking about being tied to the bed, and my cock in you, the whole time."

Jessie was doomed. Lucky her.

Dan wasn't entirely correct. Distracted by catching up with their friends and eating tasty, garlicky tidbits, Jessie managed to push erotic images to the back of her mind for a few minutes at a stretch.

Whenever she caught a glimpse of her wrists, though, she clenched as she imagined them straining above her head, bound to the headboard by the same scarves, or tied together behind her back. She'd flash to thoughts of what Dan might do to her when she was deliciously captive, or dream of being more firmly restrained, legs spread-eagled as well, so she'd feel open, vulnerable, helpless by choice and not wanting to be any other way.

Jessie's nipples would perk, her clit would start to ache, her pussy would throb.

And then Steve would pass the *cerdo Ximenez* or Mary would ask her to pass the *gambas al ajillo* or the flavor of the *chorizos diablillos borrachos* would explode all over her tongue, or someone would start telling a funny story, and she'd forget, for a minute or two, about what was to come.

Just when she thought she was safe, as they were all busily talking about what might be in a particular sauce, Dan ran his fingernail, delicately, gently, along the edge of the silk band on her left wrist.

Her wrists weren't normally an erogenous zone, but they lit up at his touch. She swore she felt little tongues of delicious, erotic fire licking where he touched, then the same tiny tongues laving her nipples and circling her clit. The light silk felt, suddenly, like heavy leather cuffs, or at least how she imagined they'd feel. Maybe even polished stainless steel ones, something straight from some of her kinkier fantasies.

The innocent necklace she wore, a BELIEVE IN MAGIC pendant on a light silver chain, morphed in her mind into a steel collar. She imagined herself a helpless but happy slave, on display in public because it amused her master.

And god help her, her panties flooded.

"Earth to Jessie. Come in, Jessie," Mary teased. "Or Dan? Would one of you stop being all lovey-dovey and pass me the sangria?"

While Jessie passed on the half-full pitcher, Dan kept stroking her wrist. Jessie hoped that any blushing could be passed off as mild embarrassment at being a space muffin.

When Steve asked, "You guys up for trying a few more tapas? Half-price, remember," Jessie answered, "I'm all set" at the same time Dan chimed in with a yes that, to Jessie's ears, sounded a little too enthusiastic. Suspiciously enthusiastic. *Teasingly* enthusiastic.

At least he turned down Mary's suggestion to continue the evening with cocktails at their place.

Dan stroked her wrist all the way back to the car.

"Hold out your hands," he said once she was buckled in.

No; he commanded.

Jessie wasn't used to hearing that tone in his voice, for all their games, all Dan's sexy Ideas. Right now, the silk and steel in his voice made her all the more aware of the symbolic silken bonds on her wrists. She obeyed, picturing again the sexy slave girl of her fantasies.

Deftly, Dan untucked the ends of the two scarves. As he knotted them together, binding her hands in her lap, she held her breath. Her body throbbed with need.

"Now you're my prisoner," Dan whispered. "All night long."

She clenched and shuddered with hot, helpless pleasure, almost but not quite an orgasm. So close to release... She raised her hips, curving her pelvis up, and opened her legs. "Please touch me." Her voice sounded alien, throaty and needy.

Dan shook his head. "Not yet. Not until I get you home." Holding her bound wrists, he kissed her on the forehead. That soft, almost chaste caress provoked another fiery wave, another near-orgasm.

The drive home took only fifteen minutes, but for Jessie it might have been fifteen seconds or fifteen hours. She stared at her hands, squirmed against the colorful fabric connecting them, not to free herself but to be sure she couldn't. The quick tie allowed play between her hands—she thought she could loosen the knot if she had to—but she wasn't going anywhere without an effort she didn't want to make. Soft, sensuous, secure, the scarves held not just her hands but her whole body and some portion of her soul.

When they reached the condo building, Jessie assumed Dan would untie her hands until they were safely inside. Instead, he left her to cross the parking lot and go into their townhouse with her hands tied in front of her. She couldn't help imagining someone running into them in the parking lot: Jan Feldman the librarian, or the retired minister from 6B, or better/worse yet, the hot young black guy, the new basketball coach at the college, who'd moved in next door a few months ago. No one was around, as it turned out, but the thought of being caught in bondage turned her on so much she was staggering by the time they got in the door.

Dan placed her hands on his crotch. Hot, hard, straining against his jeans, his cock seemed as captive as her hands. "You're not the only one," he said. "I've been like this on and off all night. I feel like a teenager."

"But unlike a teenager, you know what to do with that hard-on."

"Yeah. I do. Bedroom, now."

He didn't need to say it twice.

As he untied the knot that fastened her hands together, Dan's hands seemed more awkward than they had before, as if arousal was making him clumsy. Jessie moved to undress, but Dan shook his head. "Let me." His voice was deeper and harsher than usual—more erotic, even though she loved his normal voice.

She could definitely get used to this, at least in the bedroom. Impatient, though, she was glad she'd opted for a simple T-shirt and skirt, and a front-clasp bra, making the whole process faster.

Wearing only her drenched panties, she lay down on the bed. Her breathing was irregular and she couldn't seem to control it. Her heart was racing and that fast pulse beat in her clit as Dan drew her panties over her hips and down her legs. She opened her legs, begging with her body because she couldn't seem to form words. "Not yet," Dan soothed.

No, of course not yet, not until he tied her hands to the brass headboard.

The scarves weren't long. She doubted he could make a completely secure knot. But once Jessie's hands were stretched over her head and tied, she felt as effectively immobilized as if he'd locked her in place with steel. Steel: there was that image again, of steel cuffs and a steel collar.

Language seemed far away, but Jessie made herself speak. "I keep imagining metal cuffs and a collar. And maybe a spreader bar or something, like we saw on that website."

Dan's laugh came from his cock. "Hot image, but I like knowing I get us both to this state without anything that fancy. Spread your legs, Jessie. I don't feel like looking for more scarves, so I want you to imagine I've tied your ankles to the bedposts. Don't move until I tell you to." Her legs were already open. How could they not be, excited as she was, hot as she was for Dan's touch, his tongue, his cock? She spread them wider and imagined them forced open, locked in place, soft, body-warmed silk on her ankles or even cold steel. "You just got wetter," Dan said, and she nodded. He ran two fingers over her slick, swollen lips, making her mewl with need, then brought them to her mouth.

She sucked eagerly, tasting herself, imagining Dan's cock in her mouth, basted with her juices. From the noises Dan was making, he was imagining the same thing.

When he withdrew his fingers, long after they were clean, she raised her head, trying to follow, but she could only go so far with her hands tied to the bed frame, her legs free, but effectively bound. Dan chuckled.

Then he began to strip, slowly and teasingly.

Jessie always appreciated Dan's body, but now, unable to touch, she looked at him in a new way, seeing the play of muscles under his skin, the dusky color of his tight nipples, the faded scar on his thigh from a childhood mishap, the slight curve to his straining cock and the way it rose so strongly out of its nest of pubic hair.

Unable to move more, she undulated on the bed. A noise came out of her throat, halfway between a purr and a growl. She couldn't remember the last time she was this turned on, this needy—and Dan wasn't even touching her, except through the silk ties on her wrists.

She clenched and unclenched her fists, wanting to beg but unable to remember how.

Finally, naked and erect, Dan lay over her. His hot mouth closed over her nipple as his cock teased at her clit. Ripples of sensation ranged from her breast and her sex, meeting, she thought dimly, somewhere around her heart and filling that, too, with heat and need. She bent one knee, pushed up against the teasing, tempting hardness of his cock. "Not yet," he said, his mouth still full of her nipple, and pushed her thigh until she straightened her knee again.

He suckled at her until her head swam, brushed at her clit and the opening of her cunt until she was squirming and begging in a language that predated English by millennia, something so primal she figured a caveman would understand it—although he might do exactly what Dan was doing and pretend not to hear it.

When she reached the point that her attempts at speech degenerated into laughing and sobbing simultaneously, Dan poised his cock inside her pussy. He pushed in just enough to let her know how empty she was and remind her how well he could fill her. She tried to raise her hips, but there was only so far she could get without moving her legs and she couldn't move her legs. She could feel the restraints on her ankles, almost as real as the silk around her wrists. But she needed… she needed.

She couldn't plead, couldn't touch the man who teased her, couldn't do anything but receive the tormenting pleasure. She was a prisoner, and she couldn't remember why she might want not to be one. Waves of sensation crashed over her, dizzying, tormenting, magical.

Dan thrust deep into her. "Now," he roared, "now!"

She shattered, sobbing, into a million pieces. Dan's weight, his heat and the rhythm of his cock driving into her kept pushing her higher and higher, but the silk kept her safe, kept her from flying away altogether, and getting lost.

"Your legs are free, love," he said, his voice sounding almost as shattered by lust as he felt. "I want to feel them around me." So she slinked one leg over Dan's hips and bent the other so she could push against him, meeting thrust with thrust. The movement tugged at the silk ties at her wrists, and that in turn tugged at her clit. She convulsed again, screaming Dan's name. Her cunt tightened, clasped at him.

Dan started to say something, but it came out as a wild roar. He thrust harder, deeper, three more times, then collapsed. "Sorry," he grunted. "A little quick."

"Silly man," she whispered into his hair, surprised she could talk even that much. "Hard and fast was perfect."

With his last bit of focus, Dan untied her wrists from the bedpost. When he went to unwrap the scarves from around her wrists, though, Jessie just shook her head and said, "Leave them."

Let her sleep in that silken bondage overnight. They might want to play again in the morning, and Dan would keep his captive safe.

CHAPTER SEVEN

NAUGHTY, NAUGHTY—
SPANKING

I do quite naughty things now. I do like to be a bit sexy.
—KYLIE MINOGUE

S panking is a fetish in and of itself. Yes, the theme can slide sensu-
ally into a story with bondage or blindfolds or role-playing. But
spanking is so enjoyable, the act deserves to be paddled—I mean,
punished—I mean, *praised* singularly. Spanking is a concept dear to
my heart (as well as other regions of my anatomy), and I have dedicated more stories than I can easily tally to the concept. I do tend to
lose count when the strokes begin to fly.

If the subject makes you sit on the edge of your seat—whether as
the potential spanker or the spankee—be sure to proceed with care.
Safe words come in handy when "no" or "stop" lose their meaning.
(And over a lover's knee, many words lose power.)

But how do you start? Of all the fetishes I've written about, spanking is one of the most erotic to watch on video. Check out the different sexy movies dedicated to the theme to give yourself an idea of the multitude of ways to incorporate spankings into your world. You may find that you like the views from the rear, or the images of a tearful receiver. Then page through these spanking snippets to see if any leave you either craving a well-paddled bottom, or a bottom to paddle.

If you do decide to spank your way to pleasure, pay attention to small details, like the knickers in my short story called "The Prize":

I did what he said, bending over the edge of his desk, holding my body steady on my straight-locked arms. Charlie stood behind me. He lifted my skirt. He saw my panties. He touched them. Silky and pretty and red.

He pulled them down himself. Dragged them down my thighs. Let them fall around my ankles. And then he started to spank me. Hard. His hand meeting my naked skin to the rhythm of whatever music was playing in the bar. Something fast.

He spanked me until I could feel the heat in my skin, and the wetness between my thighs. Spanked me to that steady beat of rock 'n' roll music. I stared at the clutter on his desk, saw the whiteness of the papers, but the red of the pens. Only red pens. Saw the picture on the wall behind his desk. Red.

"The Last Goodbye" is a spanking story I wrote that takes an over-the-knees position:

"Over my legs, girl," he hissed. "Now."

I bent myself into the proper position, felt his warm hand lifting my tiny skirt, felt him watching me. He pressed the paddle against my panty-clad ass, letting me feel the weight of it, before he landed the first blow. I sucked in my breath, but remained silent. It was different from the belt, but not worse. He began spanking me more rapidly, pausing only to pull my black satin bikinis down my thighs, leaving them on me, but baring my ass. The pain intensified immediately, and tears wet my eyes, but I still didn't cry out. I wasn't trying to test him. This wasn't a game.

I didn't know how to do what he wanted. Not without sounding phony. Not without being fake.

In my story "OTK," the Dom understands the sub's boundaries, and pushes on them:

Jack was a master. Plain and simple. He knew how to create a rhythm in which I was momentarily lulled into believing I could handle the punishment. And then he would land a startling blow, wringing a gasp or cry from me, making me lift up slightly before catching myself and lowering my body back into the proper position.

I didn't count. He didn't ask me to. He simply paddled me until he got what he wanted. First, I held my body as still as possible. And then, I squirmed, unable to stop, and he kept me in place easily, gripping my sore wrists in one hand and pinning them in place at the small of my back. And finally, he won the tears of submission, when I simply pressed my face against the cool leather sofa, and cried.

Make the most of spanking sex. Dress for the event like the character in "Spring Cleaning" by Samantha Mallery:

When we have spanking nights (which usually come when we're cleaning the kitchen because of the plentiful wooden spoon paddles), I know to put on a pair of my sweet, lace-edged panties.

Play with different implements. Here's a scene with a belt by Xan West from "Nervous Boy":

I slowly take off my belt, knowing his ears are attuned to the sound of the buckle being released, of leather pulled through denim. I fold the belt in half, twice, and snap it, watching him twitch.

The leather bites into him. The belt brings me to a ravenous place. I want to open him up. I want to rip him apart. I want to be inside him. Now. I never take out my belt unless I'm sure I'm going to fuck, because it does this to me every time.

"Take it boy. Yeah that's it. Scream for me. Just keep taking it. I know you can do it. Show me how strong you can be."

Each hit ramps it up. Each welt a badge of strength. He rides on it, grounded in pride, sure of himself now. I growl as I concentrate on one spot. I want to ram into him so hard. I claim him with the belt instead, striking out with the bite of it, waiting for the moment when I allow myself to fuck him. We both grunt with the last blow.

Vida Bailey takes us up a notch with a fantasy about a cane from "Favorite," written expressly for me:

"What's your favorite one?"

He's sitting at his desk, chair pushed out. I'm standing at the door, blushing.

"You know the one."

"Hmm?" He raises an eyebrow. He knows the one. He loves this. I sigh and his brows knit in a slight frown.

"The one when I'm over your lap in your study."

"This study?"

"Yes." He nods for me to go on.

"The one where I've been bad. And you spank me. You spank my ass red."

"And then what happens?"

I blush deeper and hide my face against the doorway. He waits.

"Then you tell me to reach into the drawer. And take out the lube, and the plug. And you part my cheeks and…lubeupmyassandpushtheplugin." My heart is beating in my cunt.

"What happens then?" I'm drowning in my pulse, it's roaring in my ears.

"Then I bend over your desk and hold on."

"And?"

"And the cane."

"Ah, the cane. With the plug in. And how do you feel about that, Lucy?"

I hate it, it terrifies me, it hurts too much. And sometimes I sweat and dream about it, but I'm always too scared to ask you for it. But you always know when I need it. I shake my head.

"Sir." My breath is a whisper. He smiles.

"And after the cane?"

"You take the plug out and you fuck my sore, red, spanked, caned ass, Sir."

He walks over to me and takes my face in his hands.

"Oh, I do."

Red comes in so many shades. So do spankings. Experiment. Lift the paddle. Bend over the sofa. Count the blows. Take the fantasy where you need it to go.

TANTALIZING TIPS

- Submit to reading a book of sizzling spanking stories, such as Rachel Kramer Bussel's *Cheeky Spanking Stories* and *Bottoms Up: Spanking Good Stories* (Cleis Press).

- Employ household items rather than traditional paddles. There's nothing like the smack of a wooden spoon, the crack of a leather belt, or the sting of a hard-backed brush for a spontaneous spanking.

- Have a spank test (rather than a taste test). Gather up a variety of implements to see which ones make your spanko heart go pitter-pat.

BENEATH THE SURFACE

SOMMER MARSDEN

I think you need to let me put it in you for a minute." He says this to me with a wry grin and I want to appear affronted. Offended. Shocked.

I'm not. My body betrays me by sending out a rush of arousal. Nipples spike, stomach dips, pussy grows wet. I swear I can feel my eyes dilating and my pulse jumping like a cornered rabbit in my throat. My fingers are clutching cut-up vegetables, my mind is on measurements and the final head count. I'm frustrated, anxious and frazzled. I stare.

"I know you're busy, though, so just for a moment."

"I'm not…ready," I lie. Why do I always do this to myself when he surprises me this way? Why do I never just say, *Yes, dear fucking all that is holy yes! Fuck me now. I'm ready. No preamble is fine.* Why do I always insist on the buildup?

Derrick reaches out to capture my hard nipple through my worn-out UCLA tee. He pinches hard enough that my tongue roams over my lips to lick away the dryness. Pleasure and pain tangle, grapple, fight to the death and on that final bit of pressure pleasure wins. My pussy goes from wet to soaked; my need to have him now has become overwhelming. That fast. That easy. I drop my clutched vegetables on a pretty crystal plate because my hands are shaking.

What he just did to me—so simply and so expertly—is why. I want the dance of warring emotions. I want the teasing and the torture. I want the blips of pain that slither beneath my skin, dark needs swimming in vibrant want. Like eels beneath the surface of a sunny pond.

"Just a moment," I gasp. "But I'm not wet—"

"If you say you're not wet enough, Fiona, I'll have to spank you. Because it isn't just a lie. It's whatever lies beyond a lie."

Something twists deep inside of me; rippling waves of fear and excitement radiate out from my center. My body seems to be humming with electricity. I chew my lip as if considering and then blurt, "But, I'm not wet enough."

"Lie," he reminds me, smiling.

He is absolutely right. We both know it. It is a big. Fat. Lie. But one I need to tell.

"See," Derrick whispers pushing his big hand slowly past the meager barrier of my ratty old sweatpants. I'm catering an event. I'm up to my eyeballs in batter and flour and small delicate cheese twists and fruit and that ever-loving fucking veggie platter. I am dressed like a castoff or a college student. My dark hair is twisted up like a madwoman's. But I can feel my pulse slamming in my temples and my cheeks blushing a hot, slatternly red.

I watch his hand disappear inch by inch until he's turned his palm to me, cupping my mound, long thick finger nudging between my nether lips to brush rudely over my clit. Too short, that touch was too damn short. But then he's plunging a finger into me and my eyes are sliding shut. I'm so wet I can hear him sink a second finger into my willing cunt.

"Feels pretty wet to me," he says. His free hand yanks my sweats down around my knees, and I gasp. It's always a surprise when taunting turns to rough. And when rough turns to welcome it's even better.

"Let's see what we can do about that. I think you could be even wetter." He turns me roughly, and his broad hand connects with my ass. It makes a sharp crack that hurts my ears and fills our tiny kitchen. It sounds like someone snapping a green willow branch. I clench my teeth at the flood of pain and how it seems to curl and dance over my tender skin.

"Ouch," I whisper.

"You always say ouch," Derrick chuckles. When his hand connects again, crisscrossing the original blow, more pain lights up my tender nerve endings, but under that sharp pain is a wet and flexing pleasure. Joy. "And yet, this happens," he says conversationally, moving his hand between my legs.

The fingers that are inside me slide against my G-spot. My cunt clenches tight yet riven by his ministrations, his words, the whole damn sex-sneak-attack. He pulls his fingers free of me and reaches from behind to paint my lips with my own juices, and I turn my head to give him better access. I taste honey and spice and lust in my mouth.

"Seems a lot of naughty arousal for *ouch*."

The hand on my ass connects again and his fingers push past my lips to brush my tongue. I suck at those fingers as if my eagerness can save me. I lick them like it's his cock. In my mind it is his cock. And I'd lay a hefty wager that in Derrick's head it's the same.

I suck again and he lays another blow on the tingling real estate of my bottom. I shiver and let go. I completely surrender, letting my body hang slack over his arm. "Ouch," I say again with no real heat.

"Ouch," he laughs, stroking his palm over my lower back. His skin whispers as it glides over mine. Goose bumps stud my arms, my legs, and my nipples are nearly painful points inside my tee.

"Derrick—"

His mouth comes down my nape making those goose bumps even more pronounced and in addition all the fine hairs on my body come to attention. Energy and want tiptoe over my scalp and I feel electrified. Struck by lightning. Inside out.

"Please," I manage.

"From ouch to please in the blink of an eye. Or should I say in a palm print?"

He nudges me forward so my forearms hit the sink. A bag of flour hits the floor with a puff and coats my feet in white. All I can do is laugh. It's all so surreal. Wasn't I just driving myself mad a few minutes ago over canapés? Now my ass is singing grand opera and I'm parting my legs and presenting my ass for my husband.

"Look at that," he says, parting my nether lips and peering at me from behind. I blush at his intrusion, but it adds to the goodness of it. "As red as your cherries and definitely wet. Definitely ready," he says to me. His voice, almost malicious and yet full of adoration, sneaks up my spine making me flush hotter. Derrick drags his cockhead along my slick opening, pushes teasingly at my ass before driving back down to push just the tip into my desperate cunt.

I drive myself back, a little ashamed, but that only adds to the intense pleasure. That mortified feeling licks at my soul as I push my ass back, part my legs more, show him what he's done to me.

Another hard blow, this time on my pristine, untouched asscheek and I jump. The sudden snap of pain works through me like a shudder and I sob.

I repeat myself, completely undone at this point. "Please."

"Good girl." His finger pushes into me where I want his cock. A second finger is added and he's thrusting so that I hang my head, my untidy hair coming undone and unraveling swiftly into the sink. I sob again as he pushes those fingers—two of them, thick and slippery—into my ass. A cry rips out of me but then it's all soothed down to silence as his cock slides steadily inside me. He's stretching me and filling me until I'm full. And then he goes still.

"Still ouch?"

"No," I whisper.

"Still not wet enough?" He laughs softly.

"No. I'm wet enough."

I want him to move. I want him to thrust. I want him to fuck me for Christ's sake. But all I can do is wait, my bare toes grasping restlessly at the crimson-colored rag rug beneath my feet. I dare not move. I've done that before only to have Derrick withdraw and start again from scratch. This will go by his timetable. No one else's.

"Are you sure?" He rotates his hips a bit. Just enough to press the thrumming nerve endings deep inside of me.

His fingers move in my ass. In-out-in-out, a lazy I-have-all-the-time-in-the-world rhythm as he rolls his hips from side to side making my cunt grasp up tight. He does have all the time in the world. And he's using it to humble me. Make me crazy, make me beg.

I give him what he wants as a little cry flies off my lips and I say, "Please, Derrick. Please, please, please."

I hear him laugh and his fingers move in and out of my back hole so that I am biting my lip hard enough to taste the coppery kiss of blood. It's too much, it's too good. The pressure and the friction and the fact that it's so taboo and happens to be one of my favorite things in the world. I wish it was his cock there and that thought triggers another galloping flex of my internal muscles.

"You sure are ready. Wet and ready and in need of a break if I'm not mistaken…"

"Yes." I move back just a hair before catching myself. But I've broken the code, I've prompted him and that is a no-no. Derrick stills completely.

"You looked very tense." His hands are sliding along my bottom, his fingers tickling at my skin. He's not thrusting his cock or his fingers in my bum. He's making me suffer. Delicious suffering.

"I was."

"You'd probably like to blow off some steam."

"I would."

"Have some pleasure."

"Yes."

"Can you stand the waiting?"

"No," I sob, and he laughs again.

"Fair enough." He cracks me one good blow on my tingling bottom and I jump a bit. It all fades away, though, on that one blow because he's finally moving. Thrusting deep and hard, filling me so swiftly that I lift up off the floor but for my very tippy toes. I grip the edge of the sink and watch my hair swirl around the drain like a mermaid's hair swirling in ocean water.

I'm going to come, but I want him to know how much I needed this. How good this is. How much I love him, so I say softly, "May I?"

His voice has gone to a growl, his fingers pushed to the very top knuckles in my ass. I can feel his fingers and his cock sliding along each other through the thin barrier of my internal flesh. Just beneath the surface. There is always something just beneath the surface, isn't there?

"You may," Derrick says and I come. My eyes leaking thankful tears as my body shudders and plucks at him. Wrapping around his driving flesh like I can keep him close and hold him inside.

His free hand grips my hip and his fingers dig hard and deep into the thicker flesh there. I will wear fingerprints for days I'm sure and god, that is the best thing I can think of. The knowledge makes me come again.

"I don't know, are you wet enough to come twice?" he chuckles, but I can hear the barely there control in his voice. I can hear the cracks in his mental foundation. I can hear how much he wants to join me.

So I prompt him. I squeeze my pussy tight, and I say, "Come with me, please."

He's given me something I didn't even know I needed, and now I want him to have his. I squeeze again and again and trip myself into yet another small release.

"Fuck. Dirty fighting, sweetheart," he grunts and he's looped his arm around my waist and he's holding me close. His teeth on my shoulder making sparkles of pain bloom there and when he empties into me, his whole big body goes taut and I can feel his muscles tremble.

It's the most gorgeous feeling. The feeling of energy and release moving through the human body. Humming along in the blood, swimming under the skin. Just beneath the surface.

CHAPTER EIGHT

FANTASIES FIRST—
ROLE-PLAY

You have to learn the rules of the game. And then you have to play better than anyone else.

—ALBERT EINSTEIN

I've been a waitress, a nurse, and a bombshell. I've been a stripper, a streetwalker, and a dancer at the Crazy Horse. Trust me, I am no actor. I stutter and stammer on stage. Public speaking is my personal hell. But I love role-playing. Why? Because role-playing gives you permission to be anyone you want. And as you might have predicted, I have a wicked imagination. I'm an ace at thinking of new characters to be in the bedroom...and beyond. When I'm not creating ones from scratch, I'm embodying the characters of strangers I've seen in my travels.

Happily, you don't need much to start this sort of game: A fantasy the two of you have shared. A movie scene you'd like to make real. A passage in a book—you only need to be on the same page.

Maybe in real life you're pretty experienced. When you role-play, you can be a virgin, like the character in my story "The Girl of His Dreams":

He was shaken. He said, "I've never seen you..." then lost his train of thought, "never seen you so..."

"What?" I asked, liking being in charge of the scenario, having no problem age-playing with him. I thought of the minidresses that I'd worn in college, still boxed up in my attic. I thought of the cheerleader outfit at the back of my closet, the one I'd worn in high school and at several Halloween parties since then. If Jonathan wanted young, I could give him young.

"You're just so sweet," he said again, running his fingers over my lips, bare of their normal dark raspberry shade of gloss. I had on no lipstick, no eye shadow, my face clean and fresh. He kissed me, taking my face in both of his hands, kissing me more passionately than ever. I basked in it, relaxed against him, felt the buckles of my overalls pressing into my skin. I said, "You really like this, don't you?" leaning my body on his to feel his cock pressing against me.

He swallowed hard. He was having a difficult time admitting it.

"There's nothing wrong with a little role-playing," I said. "I can be the girl next door, outside gardening in my overalls." I bent forward so that he could see my naked breasts beneath the denim bib. I undid the buckles again and let the front of the overalls fall open. He reached forward and touched one of my small, pert breasts, and then the other. He looked like he was going to pass out.

In "A Quick Ten," I show how spanking and role-playing go hand in hand. Well, a hard-backed brush goes in one hand, but role-playing goes in the other:

He gave me two more strokes, raising the number to nine. I could tell he was going to make the tenth count, and he didn't let me down, giving me the hardest stroke of all for the finale. Tears filled my eyes and a moan rose in my throat. Then, without a word, he lifted me from his lap, threw me down on the bed on my stomach and went on his knees on the floor behind me. He kissed my reddened asscheeks, kissed along the crack between them. He thrust his tongue between my thighs and lapped at the honeyed nectar that had collected there.

And then he fucked me, opening his fly and freeing his cock, fucking me from behind so that his clothes rubbed against my hot ass. He made me come like that, the feeling of being filled complemented by the coarseness of his pants rubbing against my skin. He said, "You liked that, bad girl. Only a really bad girl would get off on that," still playing along. Still in the role.

One of the best things about role-playing is the fact that nobody is trapped. You can be one character one night, and someone new the next. Samantha Mallery writes in "Spring Cleaning":

Eleanor nodded her immediate approval. She stood on our patio, a tissue-wrapped bouquet in her lovely hands. I let her in, feeling shy, as I always do when she's in charge. It's fun taking turns this way. It gives us both the opportunity to play different roles. When Eleanor is in charge, her very appearance seems to change. She has light honey-colored hair, and freckled skin. Her eyes are a deep brown, and they seem to glow when she's in charge. They have a heat to them, and they flicker like the purple-gold flames in a campfire.

Elise Hepner's "A Shot" takes the fantasy of role-playing to a new level—outside of the bedroom.

"A shot. Tequila."

A glass slid across the bar, amber liquid coating the glossy-topped wood.

"Thanks," Hattie shifted her black curls behind one ear and glanced down—back toward the man in a black muscle-tee and low-slung jeans.

His gray eyes appraised, full mouth inching up into a half grin. The nape of her neck burned, a blush flared up her pale cheekbones. His stern nod to the half-spilled shot. With a deep breath, she knocked it back. Now the burn inside matched the heat on the outside.

"Another," she croaked, waving a ten.

He saddled closer, snatching her wrist in his icy grip. His bruising fingers wrenched a low gasp out of her lips, breasts inching forward across the bar, scraping her extra-sensitive nipples across the wood. Tender, aching, full. A shudder licked down her spine.

"I'll be the judge of that. Get back there. I'll come for you."

His other hand caressed her cheek and her pulse skittered. Their eyes locked. Her mouth watered, pussy slick, mind blank. He was sweet-scented—and devious. So right.

Did he have to say anything else?

Why not?

Hattie waited, fingers tapping the bathroom door frame. Nipples pebbled with anticipation.

Before she composed her thoughts, he shoved her back against the door. A rough clap—stung her back and ass. Her hand palmed his thick cock. His breath, a sensual tease.

"I've always wanted to fuck a bartender. Glad you hijacked your best friend's job."

"Your wish, my command, wife."

Sharon Wachsler's "Alternative Medicine" is a twist on the doctor/patient fantasy that many couples share:

I entered the dark bedroom. She was lying in an oversized T-shirt on her back with a black mask over her eyes and a cold, wet cloth on her forehead. When the sleeve of my white coat grazed her thigh, she sucked in her breath.

"You've had this migraine all day?" I asked, placing my black bag on our nightstand.

"Yes, doctor."

"The medication hasn't helped?"

"No, doctor."

"Now, because you'll try anything, you've asked for my help?"

A whisper. "Yes. I'm desperate."

"Pain specialists," I said, opening my bag and taking out gloves, lube and a small purple butt plug with a remote vibe, "have found that providing an alternative focus can distract the patient from her pain."

"Mm," she said, unmoving.

I snapped on the gloves—loudly—and she jerked. I lubed up the plug, lifted her legs and slid it in her ass.

"Oh!"

I slapped her ass. "If you relax, it will be more efficacious," I instructed, turning the vibe to low.

A soft moan.

"Lie still and focus on the stimulus," I directed. "I have to make rounds. I'll be back later to finish your treatment." I dropped a leather paddle and a condom next to her. Her hand found each in turn, and a slow smile spread across her face.

I turned the vibe to medium, eased the door shut, and whistling, headed for the shower.

Andrea Dale's "His Lady's Manservant," plays with roles in a delicious manner:

Melina tended to be a screamer, and her orgasm solidified our roles: she as the lady of the manor and I as her manservant, the besotted lover kept secret because of class boundaries.

When she rode me (of course she'd take the dominant position), my thoughts truly were for her pleasure. My hands at her breasts, my hips bucking to her rhythm, it wasn't until she was falling over the edge again and gasping, "Yes, come for me," that I was finally allowed—that I finally allowed myself—the relief I'd craved.

She didn't banish me to the servants' quarters that night, although for the remainder of my weekend she stayed in character.

As I loaded our suitcases into the car, I could only think ahead to when we'd reprise our parts…in private.

Cora Zane's "Bad Kitty" shows that you don't even need to be human when you're playing a part.

She watches me unzip my pants, and I recognize that look of majestic indifference. Sasha meows and stretches her sleek body across the unmade bed. Her red-vinyl claws rake the black satin sheets as a proper pussycat is wont to do. The little bell on her studded, leather collar is a soft chime marking her every movement. I step to the edge of the bed, hard cock in hand, and in defiance, she lies on her side and flicks her cheetah-print tail at me.

"So that's how it is, is it?"

She lifts her chin in dismissal.

"Bad kitty." I slip my finger under the edge of her collar, and pull her toward me, the motion forcing her to her knees.

Annoyance flickers in her emerald eyes.

"You know master wants his cock sucked."

To soothe her, I stroke her black hair, and reluctantly, she nuzzles her face against my hand. That's when I press the head of my dick to her lush mouth, smudging her wet, red lipstick.

She bathes my cock with the tip of her tongue then sucks me in deep.

I fuck her mouth for what feels like hours. When I'm close to coming, I tighten my hand in her hair, and Sasha digs her claws into my thighs. Moaning, I explode into her mouth. Good kitty, she licks up every drop. When she finally releases me, I'm shaking and weak—and she's grinning at me. My smug little cat who got the cream.

CJ Lemire takes a page from a fairy tale in "Princess Games":

Sleeping Beauty lies sprawled across our canopy bed, dolled out in ruby-red corset, long black skirt, and fuck-me shoes.

Acoustic guitar plays from the speakers. An orangey scent wafts across the room. Reflected candlelight tangos across the bedroom walls.

I set the ice bucket on the dresser, kiss her, take in her perfume.

Boyfriend. The one that makes her smell like she's just come from some other man's arms.

My hard-on strains against my suit trousers. Wait till my mouth gets to your other lips, sweetheart.

From the hope chest at the foot of the bed I select four lengths of rope, the blindfold, lube, peppermint oil and a pair of nipple clamps, which I toss into the ice bucket.

Anything else I might need? Once the lid's closed I can't go back, my selections are made. Perhaps the vixen has panties on, cleverly tucked under her garter straps? I add a pair of EMT scissors to my pile.

I have an hour to get Sleeping Beauty to rouse and respond. Fail, and I'm hers for the night. But if I win, and I intend to win, she's all mine.

Game on, Princess.

Now ask yourself: *Who do I want to be tonight?*

TANTALIZING TIPS

- You don't need anything in order to role-play, but costumes and other accoutrements (say a sex toy or two) can definitely ratchet up the pleasure. If you open that door in your mind, you'll find all sorts of unusual uses for rubber gloves, ties, ace bandages, spatulas...

- If improvisation is difficult for you, play out an erotic scene from your favorite book or movie. You might even be inspired to change the plot along the way. This can be your own fan-fic come to life!

- Play at being each other. Even without costumes or cross-dressing, take a turn...

AFTERNOON STRIP

N. T. MORLEY

It was a big house, so it wasn't totally unprecedented when Jackson's phone buzzed on the coffee table and he discovered it was his wife texting him from the top floor. There were a lot of stairs; sometimes she saved herself the trip.

About an hour ago, he'd left Helene napping in the bedroom while he came out to read. His book had taken a turn for the boring, and Jackson had just been sort of vegging out for a while. Truth be told, he was getting a little horny—as he tended to on Saturday afternoons—and so he was thinking about mounting those three flights of stairs and paying his napping wife a visit in any event; there was nothing he or she loved more than an afternoon fuck when she was good and sleepy.

But then he'd heard the telltale whine of the old Victorian's pipes that told him Helene was taking a shower. Helene's showers were legendary; they could go on for upward of half an hour, so he thought maybe he would join her—but when he went back and tested the door to the bathroom, he discovered it was locked.

His wife wasn't in the habit of locking the door to the bathroom, but hey, that was her prerogative, right? So Jackson figured he was on his own for the time being. He returned to the living room and toyed with the idea of calling up some porn. But he decided to nap himself, right there on the couch. When he was awakened by the phone buzzing, he saw it was Helene texting him.

The text said: *Do u have ur wallet?*

Jackson's wallet was on the table by the front door, where he always ditched it when they entered the house. But why would he need it? Did she want him to order a pizza?

He texted back: *Y.*

Helene answered: *Small bills?*

Yeah, of course he had small bills. He always did; he was a cabdriver. It went with the territory.

He texted another *Y;* Helene responded, *Close the curtains.*

Jackson texted back: *OK,* but he was thinking, *WTF?* The curtains were already closed.

Helene had recently rigged the living room speakers to her office computer on the second floor. That was one of the many reasons Jackson hadn't been bothering to watch TV or listen to music in the living room much. Now, the speakers blared to life with Rhianna's "S&M"—the extended, extra-dirty mix.

The throbbing rhythm echoed across the hardwood floors. Even above it, he could hear the deafening *click-click-click* of very high heels on the hardwood stairway—so he was watching for her when she entered.

Those heels were loud, all right, in more ways than one. The heels were maybe eight inches; the balls of Helene's feet rested on two-inch, clear-plastic platforms, strapped in by bright red leather that also crisscrossed all the way up her perfect, freshly shaved calves almost to her knees, where they gave way to just the white stockings with the lace tops maybe two inches south of the hem of Helene's pleated plaid skirt. The lacy tops had red bows in front and back, and she wasn't wearing garters. Her tits were tied up into a white blouse knotted just under and between them, and while they often defied gravity in Jackson's mind, he had no doubt that under that blouse they were packed into a seriously aggressive push-up bra. Her nipples stood out rock hard through the see-through white material. A straight black tie dangled between them.

Jackson froze for a moment. Was she a schoolgirl or—

Helene killed the light and turned on the disco lamp she'd insisted on, over Jackson's protests. Jackson was pretty glad she'd insisted now. Her body dancing with colored lights, she sashayed across the hardwood floors easily. She had a grace that Jackson wondered at; he couldn't believe this was his wife. Her hips swung and pivoted to the music, a bump-and-grind that left very little mystery as to what was on her mind—or what she wanted to be on her "client's" mind.

The loud music shrouded Helene's joyfully singing along as she swung and pirouetted around the room toward a gaping Jackson. The skirt was pleated, not tight, so she had quite a bit of mobility. But there really wasn't very much to it. There were inches of creamy pale perfect flesh between her stocking tops and the skirt. If Jackson had happened across a grainy JPG of this woman on the Internet, he would have popped a boner instantly. He sure as hell popped one now.

Jackson stared at his dancing wife. He grabbed his wallet. He took out a stack of ones, fives, tens; he resisted the urge to count them, and just held them up where Helene could see them. She blew him a kiss, bent over, lifted the skirt. She worked her ass obscenely back and forth in time with the music. A sickening swarm of disco dots sparkled over her perfect ass. Her hand dipped down into her panties, tugged the G-string to the side and gave him a filthy little look as she tapped her sex with her long-nailed fingers. He saw she was shaved. Thank heaven for Helene's long showers, he thought.

Jackson leaned out, waving a five. Helene let him slide it into her G-string, slowly, sensuously caressing his fingers with hers as he tried not to touch her pussy—because you weren't supposed to, right?

He didn't. He got the five in her G-string without going too far, while his dancing wife waved her pussy in his face and smiled. He had a twenty ready in his other hand. He showed it to her, saw her eyes light up. She backed her ass up, closer—close enough that Jackson could smell her, smell it, smell her pussy and her ass and the perfume she'd dotted on her thighs. He felt dizzy and drunk and wished he had a highball like in a real strip club; he needed one. With the twenty in play, Helene brought her ass very close to Jackson's face. He slid it in easy, closer to her pussy this time, and once it was seated, Helene reached back with her naughty little fingers and pulled her husband's hand in deeper. He felt the smooth perfect texture of her sex against his hand; his hard dick throbbed ever harder.

He barely got a touch; she was moist, but she was *working*. She gave him just as much as he deserved for twenty dollars—then she pirouetted off across the room and started stripping.

If there was not very much to the skirt, there was even less to the top. It had been a white blouse, once upon a time, but she'd tied it up tight under her upthrust tits. There were four buttons secured between the knot of the black tie and the knot of the blouse. Between the buttons, the tight blouse gapped. The whisper of a cranberry-lace push-up bra spilled out, and Helene's breasts spilled out of *that*. As she loosened the tie and unbuttoned the top, Jackson's eyes widened. He waved a twenty. Helene gave him a friendly sneer, singing along with the music. She left her blouse half-undone—her cleavage now maddeningly visible—and pulled the barrette from the back of her head, releasing her cascade of blonde hair—no pigtails for this school-girl. She whipped her hair everywhere and leaned in tight and hard against Jackson to rub her tits in his face.

She smelled so perfect—trashy perfume, pussy, sweat, shower, laundry detergent. She rubbed her tits in his face and mouthed, "You wanna see more?" with her eyes on the twenty. Jackson did. He held up the twenty and she finished undoing her blouse. She leaned down, cleavage in his face, and Jackson eased up the twenty. He pushed it into her bra, and Helene lost the blouse in one slutty shimmy motion, while she rubbed her cleavage all over his face.

It was a new song—2 Live Crew or some shit, Digital Under-ground, maybe, some kind of hot, hard hip-hop thing about fucking and sucking. On the top, Helene just wore the cranberry push-up bra and the straight black tie. She spun away from Jackson, leaving her husband staring open mouthed. The twenty disappeared. Helene bent over again and showed him her thighs, her ass, her pussy. Her hips worked wildly, mimicking intercourse; if she'd done this routine in a strip club somewhere, Jackson figured she'd either find herself buried by a shower of money or locked up in a county jail cell.

Helene worked through a furious routine as Jackson watched and waved bills. After the hip-hop there was the blaring explosive throb of White Zombie's "More Human Than Human," to which Helene went bat-shit crazy. She loved this damned song. She didn't earn a single bill while she flipped out on the floor, facedown, ass up, hips pumping in a fascinating mimicry of some nasty, hard fuck. She didn't earn a single bill, but Jackson never stopped waving them, or watching his wife go to town. By the end of it, she was soaked in sweat and all but dripping.

She was so hot, in fact, that she very badly needed to lose her skirt when some crappy '80s rock shit started. Jackson couldn't stand this kind of cracker shit, but he didn't really care. Helene wiggled over to

Jackson and sang along; something about cherries, pie, sweet—whatever. She looked so goddamn good dancing to it that it almost made Jackson like the song—but not quite. He was thoroughly distracted, though, by very badly wanting his wife to get naked.

Helene did—but slowly, torturously, teasing him.

She gave up the skirt in installments, slowly working it down her slightly spread legs while she rubbed her ass in Jackson's face and he reached around and rubbed bills over her belly, her thighs, her tits. Every now and then, she'd check the denomination and put her hand on his, guiding it down or up into her G-string or her bra. Every five he slid into the front of his wife's G-string got him another inch; every five he slid into her bra got one bra strap down or one tit out of its bra cup.

When her bra finally came off, she shoved it in Jackson's face. He took a deep breath and smelled her essence on the cranberry lace.

Helene was practically naked, now—and yet not naked at all. She wore nothing and everything—stockings, G-sting, and those shoes with the crisscross leather straps on up to her stockinged knees. She looked filthier than Jackson had ever felt she looked when she was stark-raving naked, beautiful and tender, pale and perfect sprawled across their bed. There, she looked pure, innocent, shameless and very, very married. Here, she looked like a whore, like a slut, like a bitch if she had to be, like a money-hungry working girl who would go as far as she needed to get every soft, moist bill out of Jackson's hand. She looked like the kind of girl out to take what she could get and give what she had to and clearly planning on getting everything while giving as little as possible.

She had her husband in the palm of her hand.

The music still blared; she still danced. But Helene had apparently reached her tease-and-denial limit; she was all over Jackson. Her G-string still stuffed with bills, she crawled on him and gave him the unsolicited lap dance of his life, grinding her body all over him, her ass on his cock, her hair in his face, her tits and her hands all over him—never quite in the places a stripper couldn't go…but always damn close. Just like a real stripper…only better.

Because Jackson was getting to the point where he was going to grab his wife and take her to bed whether she liked it or not.

And he was pretty damn sure she'd like it.

But for one and a half songs, he obediently sat on his hands while she danced herself into a frenzy atop him, sweating everywhere. She went farther and farther with every hard grind against his body, until her bare tits were slippery with sweat and he couldn't stop himself from taking her nipple in his mouth.

And here was where the two of them lost it; they couldn't play the game anymore. Her hands seized his and guided them up to her tits. He played with her nipples while she kissed him, kissed his ear, his neck, groped hungrily after his shorts.

Then she was down, out of Jackson's grasp—down on her knees, and his cock was in her mouth before he knew it. He could have spilled himself into her mouth with barely any effort, but Helene was too much of an expert to let that happen. She teased him, letting him run his hands through her hair while she sucked his balls, pinched his cockhead, held him right there on the edge. She knew exactly when her husband had cooled; that's when she slid her way up his body and guided his cock to her smooth-shaved pussy.

A real stripper would have used a condom—even if she was the kind of stripper who did clients in the VIP room for an extra two hundred dollars. She would have rolled a condom over a stranger's cock—even in the shadows, even when the bouncer had been tipped to look the other way. Helene didn't do that—but then, she also hadn't upped the price before putting out. She just pulled her G-string out of the way and slid her smooth, perfect puss down over her husband's cock, teasing him with soft firm strokes of his cockhead up and down in her slit. Her eyes crossed and sometimes rolled back as she tried to stay grinding to the music, but pretty soon she couldn't stand it. She slid his cockhead to her entrance and sat down on him hard.

She rode him slowly, kissing him, making eye contact, biting her upper lip hard and whimpering so loud he heard her over the music. It was an excellent position—the head of his cock hit that spot she so very much loved. She rubbed herself furiously, her finger making eager circles on her clit as Jackson's hands dug into the flesh of her soft round ass.

She came an instant before her husband did. She shivered and spasmed atop him. Then she looked in his eyes and begged him for it: "Please, baby. Give it to me." Jackson couldn't hold back. It only took a few more thrusts; he lifted his hips to plunge deep into her.

Then he came in his wife, as the music peaked.

Later, the two of them cuddled on the couch, exhausted and still dripping sweat. The living room smelled like her.

"You really got a workout," Jackson said.

Helene kissed him hungrily and said, "Not as good as the workout I'm gonna give you."

They ended up ordering pizza after all, and Helene had to pay. She'd earned every dollar her husband had on him. But then he earned it right back.

CHAPTER NINE

BACK-DOOR MAN—
ANAL

Games lubricate the body and the mind.
—BENJAMIN FRANKLIN

We've had the bondage, the blindfolds, the oral and the spankings. Now we're ready for anal. Right? And honestly, who's not into anal? Sure, people will blush or turn away. They protest too much and turn bright pink. But if you do a quick search on the Internet for "anal," you'll come up with 1,020,000,000 results in about two seconds flat, starting with the Wiki page for Anal Sex, and moving right on to what women love and hate about anal, definitions of anal, and how to have anal for the first time.

If this is a new-to-you concept, my advice is to take things slowly. Foreplay is key with anal sex. Explore your fantasies before you even reach for the Astroglide. How? Simple. Moisten the tip of your index finger, part the covers of a few popular books, and dive into the tight, velvety tunnel of anal erotica.

Not to come off as a wiseass, but I consider myself a bit of an expert on the subject of anal erotica, having edited *Luscious* (which may be the first anthology ever to be dedicated solely to anal sex) and piloting the Annual Anal Erotica series (*Kiss My Ass*, *Bad Ass* and *Smart Ass*). Forget Googling, I have 775 files on my hard drive dedicated to anal sex.

My stories focus on partners discussing the concept, like in this clip from "Connecting," where one lover confesses a sex dream:

"You told me that you wanted me to fuck your tight little virgin asshole."

"I said that?" she was panting, shutting out the picture by closing her eyes. Seeing a completely different image behind closed lids.

"Yes," he said, "you filthy little slut. You said, 'Please, Chas. I'll hold it open for you. Put the head in and fuck my ass.'"

They'd never done that before. She'd never spoken like she had in his dream. He'd never indicated that he wanted to try anal.

"Did I like it?"

"I didn't fuck your ass right away. I made you wait for the big event."

"Why?"

"So you'd be really desperate."

"What did you do first?"

"I took you in the bathroom and bent you over the edge of the tub. I spread shaving cream between your asscheeks and shaved you so you were completely clean and neat back there. Then I showered you off and licked your back door until you were moaning the way you do when I eat your pussy."

"God," Jennifer sighed. "Oh fuck."

In my story "Antonia's Beast," a woman describes her first anal-sex experience to her best friend and an eavesdropping stranger:

She tells it like she's telling a bedtime story, in a low lilting voice that has a rhythmic pulse to it: They've never fucked like that.

She hesitates, makes herself continue. They've never had anal sex. He's never tried, and she certainly wouldn't have suggested it. But his fingers slowly start to probe her back door. His pointer and his middle finger push their way inside this tightest of openings. She sighs. She clings to his leg. She lets him continue. He makes circles with his fingertips as he delves farther. Antonia's breathing speeds up. She feels as if she's going to pass out. She begs him to stop, but she doesn't mean it.

Marcus is gentle, but persistent. He lubes her up and massages her until she is relaxed and ready. More than ready, dying for it. She is inexperienced and she wants suddenly to be experienced.

Sometimes simply talking about what's going to happen is enough to get a person going. In Clarice Alexander's "Blue Denim Pussy," the anal doesn't happen on the page. It's coming:

When she opened her eyes, Colin was still helping—helping her take off her jeans and folding them into a neat square. "We'll get these," he said. "Because if you didn't guess from my response, I like them."

Then he was turning her, hands flat against the mirror, his body behind her, letting her feel the promise of his cock pressed against her ass. Letting her know with a single look at her eyes in the mirror exactly what was going to happen next—

In "Nobody's Business," by Dante Davidson, the character is brutally up front about his anal desires:

I gotta admit it. I have this thing for ass-fucking. Am I a pervert? Maybe. But I don't care. If it works for me and my lover, then it's nobody else's business, right? Don't ask, don't tell—you know what I'm saying? The truth is, I like every part of the equation, from checking out a pair of well-packed jeans, to revealing the naked haunches of a new lover, to slip-sliding my tool inside that tightest of entryways. I collect experiences, returning to my favorites over and over again in my mind. These images are better than fantasies, because they're real.

In "Fast Boil," Vida Bailey discusses anal foreplay through the use of lube and a butt plug:

He dresses faster than me. I'm still in a towel when he sits on the bed and pats his chalk-striped knee. Over I go, damp pussy pressed to his hard thighs. He's bare-chested. I'm a welter of nervous excitement because I know what's coming when I'm all freshly clean like this. I know where the fingers pushing their way between my thighs and stroking my cunt are going to go next. I smell the clean scent of new wetness as it coats his fingers. It sounds slick and loud as he spreads it against my soft skin, up between my cheeks, and slides his finger round and round my asshole. He presses on it, chuckles at the give there. I'm dying, because he can see how much I want it, because I want it so much. Need churns in my abdomen, my cunt throbs, my hips thrust.

The sensation of the cold, slick lube is almost foreplay enough; his finger slips right into me. He pushes the fingers of his other hand into my mouth and I suck them as he adds another to my ass and fucks me. I'm waiting for the plug and it's the big one, it's intense. I squirm and bite him, and when he smacks me, my ass opens and lets it slide right home. He strokes me while I writhe on him. Then he stops and sends me to stand in the corner, to wait and want and burn.

Andrea Dale moves us onward to anal beads in this scene from "Paying It Forward":

"Now the beads," she said. Did she sound like she was begging? Maybe she was, just a little.

He greased them up, carefully slipped them in. She shivered, savoring the sensations, each little pop of pleasure ratcheting her arousal higher.

She rolled off the pillows onto her back, spread her legs. Simon knew what to do. Lips and tongue and fingers, tasting and teasing, flicking and sucking. He even tugged on the string, smart boy, and she clenched and released around the beads.

Thighs tensing, belly quivering, teetering on the edge, she moaned, "Pull them out."

As they blipped out of her, one by excruciating one, she came.

In "Smokehouse," Sommer Marsden takes us all the way into the realm of anal sex from the receiver's point of view:

I do it, grinding my palm to my clit and pushing my fingers into my cunt as he moves into me, deep, deeper, deepest. He's cussing like a sailor now, trying to hang on. Neither of us ever lasted long with anal. It was so hot, so intense, so bad, so everything to us that it never lasted long.

We try to make this last. Moving together, moving in tandem, silent but for the rush and roll of our breath in the small structure as the rain whooshes a backbeat and a crack of thunder somewhere far off echoes what's going on in my chest. The turmoil, the pleasure—the need.

My fingers rub his cock through the thin and magical membrane that separates my two holes, and he makes a dark and secret noise that sets me off. I can't catch myself before I'm coming and chanting, "Oh, Jason. Oh, baby. Oh god, I mi—"

But then I do catch myself, and he finishes coming with a panting kind of roar that almost sounds tortured. Both hands are firmly on my hips now, his fingers denting my skin with an aggressive possessiveness.

And time stills. All of it.

Whether you only play with words, or choose to work up to an actual anal event, lube your mind and the ass will follow.

TANTALIZING TIPS

- Invest in a good lube. In this case, there's no such thing as too slippery.

- Make a game out of anal. Let your partner know that you're in the mood if you leave a red ribbon on the door handle, or play a special song, or ring a bell. (That might turn Pavlov on his head!)

- Anal and spanking go well together. Start with a good spanking and follow with a raucous anal encounter.

THE FINAL FRONTIER

JUSTINE ELYOT

I knew Luke was an arse man before we even got together. He had that poster of the tennis player lifting her skirt to show her bum on the wall of his room in college. It was retro even then, and we used to tease him about it, or accuse him of sexual objectification of women if we weren't in a good mood.

"What can I say?" He'd shrug. "I'm an arse man through and through."

We lost touch for a while, scattering to the corners of the globe after graduation, but one summer at a mutual friend's barbecue, there he was, hogging the sausages. At university we'd both had other partners, but it hadn't stopped a kind of sly, breathless flirtation going on whenever we were in the same room.

Now that we were both single, it seemed inevitable from that first sausage joke over the hot coals that we would end up together. And so we did, smooching at the end of the garden when everyone else had retired indoors. As he kissed me, his hand reached down to squeeze my bottom in its thin cotton covering.

"I've wanted to touch your bum since the day I met you," he whispered.

Not the most romantic start to a relationship, but it turned me on anyway.

I liked to dress it up for him—tight jeans for the pub, shiny spandex hot pants for the nightclubs. He couldn't keep his hands off it, following wherever it led. He particularly liked it when I wore a tiny latex miniskirt I'd bought in the goth shop in town, though I tended to save that one for the bedroom. I'd bend over, stretch that rubber tight as tight, listening behind me for the moans of agonized awe that preceded his pounce.

As time went on, I let him spank me, growing to enjoy the sound of his hand on my heating skin and the way it lit up my sex and made my juices flow. I'd never imagined I'd enjoy that kind of thing, but over his knee became one of my favorite places to be.

Another one was on my hands and knees on the bed or the floor or wherever, my spine bent, the better to thrust out my bottom, while he pounded into me, his hands scooping those generous curves.

I guess I knew the day was coming, but I avoided thinking about it. Surely it was enough that he got to see and feel and touch and spank my bottom to his heart's content. Surely this would satisfy him and he wouldn't want to...my sphincter would clench before I got as far as explicating the thought.

So it was left to him to moot the subject.

Once again I was on my knees, face in the duvet, arse in the air, naked except for stockings and suspenders, pushing back on his cock, eager to get it all inside me.

"Mm, do you want it, Lis?"

"Yeah, please."

He ground his pelvis, tried to push his cock farther in, but it simply wasn't possible. He placed his thumbs on my inner buttcheeks ___ ___em apart, something he'd done many times during sex, ___ duly alarmed.

___e placed one of those thumbs on my anus and I jolted ___dly we nearly toppled over sideways.

___m." He patted my hip but kept his thumb in situ. ___atter?"

___ching…it feels weird."

___?"

___

___ever wanted to try anal sex?"

___t."

___ight. I don't mean tonight. I mean, ever."

___w. It'd hurt. You'd never fit. And it's just…a bit

___. It's dirty, but that's good. You can make sure you're ___, if that's what you're worried about."

___ what I'm worried about. I'm just worried."

___n you on?"

___s trying hard to keep his tone neutral, not disap- ___cive. I loved him for that. I loved him anyway.

___d his question seriously.

___e discuss this face-to-face? After you've fucked me ___t's distracting me so very much right now?"

___aughed.

We fucked. Throughout the fuck, I imagined his cock was farther behind, in that secret, hidden, transgressive place. I imagined how it would look, that fat, thick thing gliding in and out of the tiny opening. I imagined how hot and nasty and helpless and dominated it would make me feel. When I came, I came harder than usual.

But if ye have bitter envying and strife in your hearts, glory not, and lie not against the truth. JAMES 3:14

As we lay together afterward, I asked him why he liked the idea.

"I've always liked it," he said. "It's my number one fantasy. I suppose because it's so perverted and forbidden. Arse—the final frontier."

He said it in a cheesy movie-trailer voice, and I giggled.

"If I have you there," he continued, "then I've really had you. For me, it's the ultimate act, it goes further than ordinary sex. It's more intimate, you need more trust between partners."

"But does it feel good?" I voiced the only real doubt that was left in my mind.

"For me it does. And the girls I've done it with—well, they said it did too."

"Right. You've done it before."

"Only with serious girlfriends."

"So with three people?"

"Yep."

I was almost sure I wanted to do it, but this thing about the three former girlfriends sparked a moment of insecurity that made me want to refuse, just to see if he would still stay with me.

"What if I said never in a month of Sundays? Would you go and find somebody who would?"

"God, Lis, no! I wouldn't force you into anything, and I wouldn't leave you just because you didn't want anal sex! It's not the be-all and end-all of my life. I just think you'd like it…and you should try things out before deciding how you feel about them."

"Shall I drink poison to see if I like it or not?"

But I was only teasing. He'd reassured me.

We set a date for a week Friday. There would be fine dining, a little inhibition-dissolving wine, then I would be buggered.

I surfed sex ed websites to find out how to make absolutely and positively and definitively sure I would be prepared for the occasion. I didn't fancy the idea of an enema but the anecdotal evidence from

squeeze my muscles, which made him notice straightaway.

"Oh, Lis, I don't think I can wait," he groaned into my hair.

I didn't think he could either. He was rock hard, pushing into my pelvic bone.

"Go and get that dress off. I'll put the food in the oven to keep warm."

I almost ran into the bedroom, discarding the heels, the earrings, the dress only minutes after putting them on.

By the time he followed me, I was propped invitingly on one elbow on the bed, one leg crossed over the other, trembling with anticipation.

"Get those legs open."

He flung off his jacket, did that sexy thing with his tie that makes it snake around under his collar then crack like a whip as it breaks free, and fell on his knees on the bed.

He grabbed my thigh, making me squeal, and then dived in, feasting ravenously and a little unexpectedly on my juicy pussy.

I suppose I'd thought he'd go straight for the main event, having waited this long, but the greedy tongue on my clit gave me no cause for complaint, especially when I came uncontrollably within a couple of minutes.

"You were nice and wet," he observed, looking down at my heavy-eyed, immobile form as he finished undressing. "Something on your mind? Something bad girls might think about? Eh? Getting you all hot and horny while you wait for me to come home and give it to you?"

"You know it."

"Yeah?" His grin was rakish. "Been thinking about that, have you? Sitting at work squirming in your seat? Thinking about what I've got in store for your arse when I get it out of that prim work skirt and onto my bed? Well, I've been thinking about it too. A lot. Good thing people couldn't see how hard I was under the desk."

"Were you as hard as you are now?" Surely he couldn't have been harder.

He squinted down at his erection.

"Pretty much. Are you ready?"

"Ready?" I shuddered. Here was the line, right here. I could cross it, or I could stay safely in the land of the unsodomized.

"Ready to take me up your gorgeous arse?"

He was practically salivating.

I answered by sitting up and slowly arranging myself on all fours, knees and elbows on the mattress, bum up high, presented in the way he most treasured. I gave it a little wiggle, expecting him to grab that lube and set to work.

Instead, he took his time. I listened to the drawer open and shut, then felt the mattress tip southward as he knelt in position behind me. My shoulders tensed, waiting for the uncapping of the lube bottle, but first he spent luscious moments kissing and caressing my cheeks, filling me with giddy lust.

I wondered for a moment if he was going to go further than he'd ever gone before and slide his tongue down between my cheeks, but eventually he turned back to the bottle and the now-familiar sensation of cold liquid oozed onto my exposed bud.

I sucked in a breath and tried not to tense my ring when his fore-finger dipped into the slippery midst, spreading it around the circle in gentle, firm revolutions. He edged closer and closer to the epicenter while I concentrated on keeping myself loose and open, letting the desire overcome the fear and take control of my body.

"Nice and relaxed," he murmured, twisting his finger this way and that, screwing it almost imperceptibly farther forward with each tiny motion. The lubricant allowed it to glide in, not quite unnoticed, but painlessly. It still felt strange and I had to work hard to ignore the frantic signals coming down to my muscles from my brain that THIS

SHOULDN'T BE HAPPENING but I breathed deeply and let him penetrate farther.

"Mm, that feels tight," he said. He stroked my flank while his finger poked and swiveled and I gave myself to the feeling of debauched abasement. "Imagine how much fuller you're going to feel in a minute, with my cock up there."

He pulled out his finger.

I whimpered a little and braced myself, but surprisingly he put his hands on my hips and nudged them sideways, indicating that I was to roll over onto my back.

I looked up at him questioningly. He responded by lifting the backs of my thighs so my legs were drawn up to my chest, bent at the knees. He placed a pillow under my bum, lifting it higher, then pulled the cheeks apart again, staring down at the target area.

"I thought you'd do it the other way," I ventured, thrown off my stride by the thought of him being able to see my face while he buggered me.

"I'll miss being able to see your arse properly," he admitted, lining the tip of his cock up with my suddenly rather tense ring of muscle. "But I'm worried if I can't see your face I'll miss a cue of some sort and end up hurting you. Believe me, we'll do it the other way next time."

"Okay," I breathed. "Okay." I made a concerted effort to loosen those muscles again, regardless of that big blunt presence right up against them.

"Are you ready, babe, are you okay? Do you need more lube?"

"No, just...be careful, yeah?"

"Of course I will. If it gets too much, you must tell me."

"I will."

I screwed shut my eyes and panted, feeling my small hole widen and stretch in its effort to accommodate this new intruder. It was never going to work, never going to fit…but it worked for countless other couples. Why not us?

I put my faith in Luke, who had done it before, after all, and let the alarm bells in my brain die down.

He slicked back and forth in the lube once, twice and then on the third attempt he put my body to its ultimate test. It stung like a motherfucker for a second or two, and then he was in.

"Oh!" I exclaimed. It really felt very unusual, as if I was so stuffed full I might burst. I held on to him, clinging, my breathing speeding up, my body threatening to tip into a panic mode.

"It's okay, it's just for a moment, it's always a bit uncomfortable the first time," he said, taking a moment to kiss my forehead.

He moved farther in and then it really *was* uncomfortable, a burning spasm shooting outward from my rectal walls.

"Push," he whispered. "Push against it."

I pushed. Within a few seconds, the pain had passed and I was left with that full-to-bursting feeling again. Luckily, I really liked that one.

Luke took everything very, very easy, watching me all the time for flickers of expression. Now, with the initial shock of penetration over, I was free to float into the headspace I'd imagined, a place of dark and primal submission, of feeling owned in every respect, taken in the most fundamental and intimate way, no longer able to say that any part of me was inaccessible to my lover.

Even at Luke's slow pace, the friction was intense, and his backward slides after each considered thrust felt like an unraveling that almost threw me back into anxiety. I didn't think I'd ever be able to get used to it. Did people get used to it?

"This is incredible," he avowed brokenly. "Your arse is so tight and hot. I'm going to fuck it all the time now. I can see you're enjoying it. You're going to get this so much, Lis."

I couldn't open my eyes. I couldn't look at him, watching me while I got my bum fucked by him. The erotic humiliation of it was sharp and sweet, but something I felt unable to share just yet.

"I'm not sure I can last…"

He put his fingers square on my clit and began to rub it, speeding me on to a climax I didn't feel quite ready for. I'd have appreciated more time to sink into the wickedness and wantonness of it. But perfect first times were rare. I was happy to settle for very good.

And very good it was, his skilled fingers joining with his cock to form a sensation so immense that I didn't know whether it was my arse or my clit that experienced the most pleasure. They seemed to become one with each other, playing on and enhancing each step toward orgasm until the final burst blinded me, throwing me into a bucking frenzy while his cock pumped furiously inside my passage.

I was only dimly conscious of Luke's orgasm, lost by then in a fog of powerful density. My own climax took a long time to wind down; I felt like a feather floating slowly to the ground.

I opened my eyes to see a blurry Luke looming over me, gasping for breath, his brow shiny with sweat, his eyes glazed, pupils flickering. He looked as if he'd arrived in heaven. I put out my hand to touch his face.

"Good?" I asked.

"So good. So fucking good. You?"

"Amazing. So different but…wow. Hard to describe."

"Yeah."

He fell on top of my chest with a grunt and rested his head on my shoulder. This caused my legs to squash right down, the upper thigh muscles straining, while I felt his cock soften inside me.

"Um." I coughed.

"Sorry." He propped himself back up. "Ready? This might feel strange. Keep relaxed."

My muscles didn't want to let him go. My body relayed the urgent message that he should stay there, rammed to the hilt in my bottom. It took a lot of deep breathing to stop the clenching and let him withdraw.

When he did, I felt an immediate sense of emptiness. My walls tightened, seeking their recent occupier and finding nothing. It was as if they felt abandoned. Poor little rectal walls. They would want him back. Sooner rather than later.

And they've had their wish. Since that night, we have embraced all things anal. We've done it in different positions, used different lubricants, introduced toys and experimented with double penetration.

"What are you going to do now, with no final frontier?" I asked him a few days after that first trip into the beyond. "Where can you go?"

"Well, it's quite a big frontier," he said, causing me to widen my eyes in indignation. "No, I don't mean your arse is big. I just mean it takes a long time to cross. A really long time. Lots and lots of attempts. In fact, I'm not sure I'll ever truly finish crossing it."

He spoke the truth.

CHAPTER TEN

BEND OVER, BF—
PEGGING

I asked my wife to try anal sex. She said, "Sure. You first."
—ROBERT SCHIMMEL

There are certain desires that don't tend to come out on a first date. When you're in the hazy, rose-hued world of getting-to-know-you, confessing to a partner that you want to slide on a strap-on and take his ass—or be on the receiving end (as it were) of that experience—is something that comes later. But if this is a fantasy of yours, be sure that it does finally come. Because pegging can open up entire worlds of pleasure.

I've buckled on the harness on multiple occasions in my work. In "Pegged," my heroine knows exactly how to please her lover:

She licked a finger, and then slowly began to circle his asshole. He stiffened, as always, before gradually starting to relax. Her lips tightened as she sucked his cock while continuing to play with his hole. Carey sighed.

When she tongued the head in rhythm with the way her finger cautiously twirled, Carey groaned. Later, he would act as if none of this had ever happened. She knew that. He would stare at her blankly with his bottle-green eyes, almost as if he'd just woken from a dream.

The narrator in my story "Plucked" is kind as she makes her lover's fantasies come true.

I kiss the welts, and Sandy groans, then I part his rear cheeks and I start to rim his asshole. I know she fucked him here. I know that. But I'm not a cold steel domme like she was. I do things my way. I make Sandy's cock all hard and ready by using the point of my tongue in his hole. I reach under him and manhandle his rod while I lick and suck. He's trembling all over, and I think again of a snake that's mesmerized the prey.

Poor Sandy, let me make it all better.

"Roger's Fault," by Eric Williams, features a ménage with pegging:

What a sight we made. Two guys in expensive work suits, perusing the aisles of marabou-trimmed nighties, edible panties, inflatable dolls, vibrators, paddles, lubricant. Roger acted casual about the whole thing, as if he shopped in stores like that every day. And then there was me, late as hell already, not knowing what the fuck we were doing there.

"Trust me," Roger said again, this time hefting a huge, ribbed purple dildo and poking around in a basket for a suitable leather harness, one that would fit your slim hips without looking foolish. He wanted to find a quality-made harness with a delicate buckle. Not too large.

"You've got to be kidding," I said.

"Elena will love it. You'll see."

"You're not buying my girlfriend a dildo."

"You're right," he agreed, and I thought I saw sanity again in my buddy's green eyes. "I'm not buying it. You are."

"There's no way."

"*Chet,*" he said, "*you can't go home empty-handed. She's going to be upset as a wildcat that you're this late as it is.*"

"*So, what?*" I asked him, incredulous. "*So I'm going to tell her to strap this thing on and fuck her aggression out on me?*"

"*Something like that.*"

And then suddenly, I understood. I'd been set up.

"Nobody's Business," by Dante Davidson, stars a character who likes to receive anal as much as he likes to give it:

Of course, I've been fucked this way, myself. I'm not one to dish out what I can't take. My introduction to the world of anal delights is clear in my memory. Not only do I possess a mental movie of that night, I remember the soundtrack, the words spoken, as well. My college girlfriend liked to talk while we fucked. Whenever we messed around, Veronica kept up a running monologue, telling me what she was going to do a split second ahead of time. She liked me because I'm the strong, silent type. I let her ramble, got into the melody, grooved on the sound of her voice.

On the night of my first ass-fucking, she asked for permission first. "Really?" I said. "You'd like that?" Yeah, I knew she was edgier than most of the coeds, but this managed to surprise even me.

She was alive with nervous energy, moving too quickly around the room, gathering her toys, her implements, promising me that I'd love every minute. Curiosity piqued, I let her bend me over the green comforter on her bed, and I waited as she got her strap-on cock wet with lube. Then she pressed her lips to my ear and hissed, "Kelly, I'm gonna take your back door."

The "taking it" is totally sexy. Elisa Sharone writes in "I Want Your Ass":

I'd asked him months before, "What are you going to do the day I show up with a strap-on?" He didn't know. He wasn't sure. He knew I wanted to give it to him, but he wasn't certain he was ready to take it. We practiced a bit, exploring more "sexy ass-play" as he liked to call it.

He'd been suspicious of my recent furtive box opening and not-so-secret stashing, so it wouldn't be long before curiosity bested him and he took a peek under the bed. Still, it surprised him when I appeared wearing a buttery-soft, dark-red leather harness and nothing else. That harness is fucking hot, with ultra low-slung slender straps that ride my hipbones and sexy metal rivet details. It's like a super-chic biker jacket for your cunt.

His erection rose as the harness registered, even though I was cockless. "You like what you see, baby?" I asked, as I climbed on the bed and knelt in front of him. "Where's the dildo?" he asked. Turned out, he was ready to take it.

Giselle Renarde makes a game of the event in "Lillian's New Toy":

I went to bed first, already wearing my naughty strap-on underneath my nightie. The lubricant was tucked secretly under my pillow. Not a secret for long, though. I was giddy, trying desperately not to smile too widely and give it all away as Frank shuffled under the covers. When the sheets began to rustle, I slipped out the lube.

Rubbing the vibrator slick with the stuff, I switched on my bad boy.

"What's that...?" Frank asked, stopping short when I slid my wet fingers along his crack. Then it was, Ohhh.

Never in my life would I have imagined tickling my husband's asshole as he jerked on his cock, but there it was! I was doing it and he was sighing at the sensation.

I held the strap-on against my husband's asshole. I didn't push right away, just let it vibrate until I got the sense he was ready to take it in. Frank didn't say a word, didn't turn around, nothing, but I knew instinctively when he could handle the purple penis.

Spooning his warm body, I eased the little vibe into his ass. He didn't have to tell me what he wanted. I knew. Grasping his love handles, I thrust into my husband's ass slowly and gently. By the speed his fist was going at his cock, I could tell he wanted it faster. I moved my hips in time with his labored breath.

Was that his heart beating a mile a minute, or was it mine?

Taking charge when you normally don't—or receiving when you're often the pitcher—can turn your bedroom upside down.

TANTALIZING TIPS

- Schedule a viewing of *Bend Over Boyfriend*, starring Carol Queen, which remains Good Vibrations' bestselling video to date.

- Peruse Violet Blue's intensely instructive how-to on the topic, *The Adventurous Couple's Guide to Strap-On Sex*.

- Play with butt plugs or dildos before going for strap-on sex.

A ROUND PEG IN A ROUND HOLE

SHANNA GERMAIN

What about this one?" I hold up one of the strap-on dildos. Realistic and not too big, but with enough length and heft that I can already imagine what it will feel like in the leather harness I bought weeks ago.

"Sarah…Jesus." Joseph's voice is hushed. If his skin wasn't so beautifully dark olive, I would be able to see him blush right now. I'm not trying to embarrass him, but we've been standing in the toy section of Slick for twenty minutes and he has done his best not to even look at the options. I know he wants this. He's told me, repeatedly, that he wants this. And, well, we won't even go into how much I want this. But I also know he's nervous about it all. Sometimes Joseph needs a gentle nudge to get what he wants.

A nudge that I'm happy to give him in the form of a pale rubber cock and a slightly raised voice. I bounce it in the air a bit, pretending I haven't seen his obvious discomfort.

"This looks like a good fit," I say. I look at him a long time. My look says: *We're going home with a strap-on, one way or another. So if you want something other than the one in my hand, now would be a good time to say so.*

Joseph moves away slightly, his voice far quieter than mine. "Maybe something less"—he touches the edge of his earlobe, then flicks a thumb over his goatee—"realistic?"

Now we're getting somewhere with his wants. I put the cock back on the shelf with the other samples and pick up a slightly smaller silicone toy. It's royal purple, with just a hint of a curve, and looks nothing like a real cock. I actually picked it out as the perfect toy the moment we walked in, but he doesn't have to know that. I've done this before, bent over the boys in my life, but it's all new to Joseph. So I want him to feel like he's the one in control, he's the one making all the decisions about what happens next.

Joseph looks at the toy, biting the side of his lip a bit. He doesn't say anything, but his breath comes a little quicker. I imagine that if I reached down, I would already feel his cock hard and pulsing beneath the fabric of his jeans. The very thought makes my own breath catch. Suddenly I want nothing more than to leave this store and have Joseph naked and bent over in front of me.

"Yes?" I ask, trying not to let my impatience show.

He drops his gaze slightly and a small smile turns the edges of his lips. "Yes, please," he says, in that soft and submissive voice that only shows up when he really, really wants something.

Oh, sweet man. Oh, beautiful man. "I love you," I say as I take his hand with my free one and squeeze. What I don't say is what he already knows, that I can't wait to bend him over and fuck him until he is moaning my name, begging me to let him come.

* * *

I wouldn't say that I fell in love with Joseph for his ass, but damn, it certainly didn't hurt. At the start, it was mostly the way he wore his jeans. And then we got together and I discovered he didn't just have a beautiful ass, he also had a deliciously sensitive one. A finger between his cheeks made him moan in delight. A little lube around his sweet spot, and he'd practically come right there.

Most guys don't have great asses. They don't even have *good* asses. They're kind of flat and white and, well, you know. Just there.

Not Joseph. Joseph has one of *those* asses. He's got Italian blood in him, so he's olive-skinned everywhere, even his ass, even in the winter. And he has these two beautiful globes, muscled and firm. Not so hard that they're not fun to squeeze. They've got just the right amount of meat to them.

He's one of those guys who are naturally gifted. Good genes and all that. But he also does these squat-something-or-others at the gym. I don't know what they are or how they work. He tells me, and I try to listen, mostly so that I can imagine him there, bending down under all that weight, the muscles of his thighs contracting, his ass wrapped in those lovely black shorts he favors. Sometimes he wears them home from the gym, not having showered, smelling like fresh salt, and I make him bend down for me right by the front door, take that beautiful ass in both hands and just knead it. All those tender, taut muscles, just begging for release. Of course I don't give it. I find the sorest spots, the ones that make him squirm, and massage until he's nearly screaming for mercy.

I say almost, of course. Because he knows how to make me merciful. And it's not by screaming. I like to hear him scream a little. More importantly, he *likes* to scream a little. It's part of what makes us such a good pair.

I'll admit—I've always liked to look at men's asses, but it wasn't until Joseph that I understood just how much of a thing I have for them. It's kind of an addiction, to be honest. But I figure since he doesn't seem to mind, I shouldn't either.

We've played a lot. Lots of kissing and fingering and lube and beginner butt plugs. Every little touch makes him happy and makes him want more. Which in turn makes me want more. Most of the time, it's amazing we get anything done besides each other.

But only recently did he admit to me that there was something he'd always wanted to try. As soon as he got out the words "bend over" and "strap-on," I was ready to jump the man's bones in a whole new way. If not for the lack of proper equipment, I probably would have.

Which is why we have just bought a beautiful purple toy that looks more like a slightly melted grape popsicle than a cock. And a lovely black leather harness that fits my curves perfectly.

It's also why this drive home feels like the longest trip ever. It's why we keep glancing at each other out of the corner of our eyes like we've got a secret. A very hot, very delicious secret. It's why we run to the house like teenagers, giggling and shoving, not knowing what else to do with our excited energy.

I make him wait. Do not ask me how I do this, because I do not know. I never have this kind of willpower. Normally, I'm a now girl, a gimme girl, but the fact that waiting is making him all antsy and nervous is somehow a reward on its own. He paces around the kitchen, putting things away, picking dishes up and setting them down, watering the plants. He doesn't look at me and yet he radiates lust like a finely honed scent. He's beautiful in his need, dressed in a white button-down and a pair of black pants. His olive skin makes a beautiful contrast with the white, his green eyes rimmed with thick black lashes. His cock makes a dramatic profile, bulging against his jeans. And his ass, well, I've already talked about that.

I watch him awhile longer, puttering. I'd say that I decided to be nice, to put him out of his misery, but really it's me who can't wait any longer.

"Come with me," I say. I'm wearing one of his favorite outfits, a crimson wraparound dress with knee-high leather boots, and I walk slow and deliberate toward our bedroom, letting him watch my ass for a change.

In the bedroom, he stands silent before me, his cock straining against the front of his pants. He's got a beautiful cock too, lightly curved with a soft, tongueable head. But I'm not particularly interested in his cock right now. I want his ass. Want is too soft a word. I *need* his ass.

"Get undressed," I say.

Joseph knows how to do this already. No touching me. No touching his cock or his nipples. No begging or pleading or asking questions. He takes off his shirt, pulling it over his head, giving me an almost-long-enough glimpse of his stomach and chest muscles working. He folds his shirt; that's his rule, not mine. His jeans are next, the lovely sweep of a leather belt through the loops and then the button-fly. Soon, he's standing before me in black boxer briefs, hands behind his back. His cock, semi-freed, strains to be released fully. A spot of precum darkens the fabric further.

I'm still fully clothed. He has the audacity to note my dress with a quizzical gaze but doesn't actually ask his question aloud. I wait until I have his full attention and then reveal myself to him slowly, letting him anticipate as I untie the wraparound and let it fall. I'm not wearing anything under it, and he releases a rough exhale of desire that makes me smile.

I practiced putting the harness on a few days ago, and as I pull it from the drawer now, I'm delighted to realize that its black leather is going to look beautiful against the purple toy. I take my time, sliding our new toy into the harness, settling the leather over my pelvis.

"Would you like to buckle the straps?" I ask.

He nods.

"The top ones first," I say. "So it stays in place while I fuck you."

I stroke his cock on those last words, and his fingers fumble a little at the buckles on my waist, his breath coming in quick pants. But he gets it perfect, and then does the same for the second set of buckles.

"Stroke me," I say.

He curls his fingers around my cock, his movement hesitant. I push into his fist and in a second, he gets the rhythm of it. Every push of his hand sends the base of the toy hard against my clit, a pulsing beat of pleasure.

"Now you too," I say.

He puts his other hand on his own cock, strokes his fist over the length of it at the same time, uttering a broken groan. God, he's hot like this. But this is just the beginning.

I put my hand over his to still his movement.

"Yes?" I ask. I want this, but I want to make sure he does too.

He nods, his eyes wide, a tiny smile at one side of his mouth.

"Good," I say. "Kneel on the bed."

"Yes," he says. He doesn't call me anything when we're fucking. Not Ma'am or Mistress or any other pet name. And when we're not fucking, I'm just Sarah. I'm the girl he loves, the girl he can bitch for not taking out the trash, the girl he holds when real life gets to be too much and I can't take it anymore. But here, in moments like this, he's all mine. And he'll do anything I say.

This is one of the parts I like best, the part where I really get to take over. I lean forward and stroke him. One hand on his cock, the other on one of his asscheeks. He moans, delightfully, little spots of color appearing across both of his other cheeks. I lick my lips, wetting them, and I can almost see his mind working. A kiss? A blow job? The not knowing makes him harder, his cock nudging against my palm, and that makes me wetter, the insides of me starting to turn warm and liquid.

His perfect ass doesn't get any more beautiful than when he's like this, and I run my palms over his muscles. A soft finger between his cheeks makes him groan softly and hang his head. I lube my fingers and the length of my cock, doing it loudly so he can hear the sounds of the lube over skin and silicone.

I give the lube a second to warm up and then I circle his asshole with my fingers, a gentle caress that sends shudders all the way up his body. His breath blows out through his teeth. At the sound of his exhale, I slide one finger into him. The way he opens and closes around me, the pucker and relax, is so beautiful it almost makes me come. I keep my focus, barely, arching my finger to fit the curve of him, finger-fucking him so slowly it's torture to keep the pace. He groans with every push, moving back into me harder each time, letting me know he's ready for more. I enter him with two fingers and then with three. He starts rocking against my fingers, pushing back hard and moaning my name.

At that, I slide my fingers from him. A soft cry of despair comes from him, and I have to smile a little. I love seeing him like this, full of need. Or more accurately, full of a need that I know I can fulfill.

"Oh my love," I say to him. "I'm going to fuck you so well you'll beg me for it again and again."

His only response is a broken groan. I rub the glistening head of the toy against his puckered hole. He whimpers a little and pushes back against the head. I enter him, just the very tip, watching him breathe, watching his body tighten and then loosen as he begins to let go. Then I stand still, letting him set the pace, watching his beautiful ass as it slides down over my cock. I'm so wet I'm afraid the dildo will fall out of the harness, but it stays secure, tight against my body.

"Ah fuck, Sarah, ah fuck," Joseph groans as he settles his ass fully over my cock.

"Yes," I say. "Fuck is just what I intend to do."

I put one hand on the curve of his ass and the other on his cock. He's gone a little soft, all of his body's attention concentrating on his ass, but I can tell my touch feels good because he shudders softly. Stroking his cock in a slow movement, I match that movement with my body, beginning an equally slow pump of my hips. He's so very fuckable like this, so very takeable, that I have to remind myself: slow, slow, slow.

But it's not long before he's speeding up the pace, grunting with each backward shove. I match his movements, jolts of pleasure riding up through me each time the cock's base pressures against my clit.

"More?" I ask.

"More," he says. "Oh god, yes, moremoremore." It's nonsense, the things coming from his mouth, but I know exactly how he feels. I don't have words and I don't have noises. I just have this pitch of pleasure, this vowelled breath that means something beyond language.

His cock is hardening again in my hand, a heavy pulsing beautiful thing that I can't let go of, even as I'm fucking him, watching myself enter and leave him, watching his muscles tighten and release with every moan of pleasure.

"Oh fuckfuckfuck," he saying, his teeth gritting so hard the words come out mashed and ground into nothings.

My orgasm is flitting around my clit, zapping little warnings of pleasure at me, and I try to hold it off, to keep focused on Joseph long enough for him to come. He's so close. His cock is pumping into my fist. His whole body is pushing back with each stroke, riding me as hard and deep as he can.

When he comes, it's with a shuddered cry of my name, his orgasm forcing his back into a tight arch, shoving so hard against my clit I see splinters of light. I come right after him, an orgasm brought on by the vision of watching myself fucking him until he comes, as much as by my own body's pleasure. It's light-headed heat and the scent of our mingled sex and a pleasure that seems to slip directly from him into me. That moment when there are no words. Breath and fuck and my heart a hundred times too fast.

After a moment, I slide from him slowly and drop on the bed next to him. Joseph gives a shy laugh of pleasure and rolls on his side to face me. We're both breathing hard, wearing huge grins. I love this feeling, as giddy as he is, both of our cocks glistening and spent.

"Good?" I ask. There's a lot more I want to say, but I haven't caught my breath yet, and all I really want to do is lie here next to him, feeling his heart beat under my palm.

"Mmm…god, so good." He touches me face, draws his fingers along my jaw. "You?"

I nod, grinning even harder.

"What?" he asks.

My face won't stop grinning stupidly, even when I try to pull my lips into something serious. "Your ass…" I say it kind of like it's a question.

"What about it?" he says.

"It's mine," I say.

"Yes it is," he says.

I lean in and kiss him, stupid happy, still all headrushy, my clit still banging out its pleasure song beneath the leather harness. I may not keep falling in love with Joseph because of his ass, but it certainly doesn't hurt.

CHAPTER ELEVEN

CROSSING YOUR T'S—
CROSS-DRESSING

Through tattered clothes small vices do appear. Robes and furred gowns hide all.

—WILLIAM SHAKESPEARE

I'll admit that my first taste of the sexiness of a man in lingerie was Tim Curry in *The Rocky Horror Picture Show*. Those mascara-drenched eyes still strike a tuning fork inside of me. I've played with cross-dressing in several of my books (in *Tiffany Twisted*, the hero spends nearly the entire book trapped in a woman's body, experiencing all the pleasures of being female for the first time). I've also plunged my boys into panties in a whole array of short stories, and I've returned the favor for my girls.

Cross-dressing can be as simple as wearing an article of clothing that is alien to you. For a man? A pair of the silkiest panties. Marco—my character in "Whose Panties?"—luxuriates in the way it feels to try on something that doesn't generally suit him:

I watched as he ran his fingertips along one of the stockings. His legs looked good, sexy. His body was very pale against the black silk. I took a step toward him, thinking that I wanted to take the place of his hands; I wanted to run my fingertips along his legs.

"There's something erotic…" he started to say, looking at his reflection in the mirrored panels around my fireplace, "something so sexy about lingerie."

I got up my nerve to walk all the way to his side, and once there I settled myself next to him on the couch. His cock was positively protruding against the silk panties, and I could see the full outline of it pressing to be free. I reached out and stroked him lightly through the silky material, and he leaned back against the couch and sighed.

I've flipped the switch and dressed my girls as males, as well, like in "Sailor Boy":

I had purchased a vintage sailor suit at a secondhand store. It was white with a black anchor on the sleeve and a musky, male smell to the fabric, even though I'd had it dry-cleaned. I hung the outfit on the back of the door while I attached the molded cock-shaped dildo to the harness, then slid the straps on and buckled the leather belt around my waist. The cock was as true-to-life as they come, as close to my actual skin color as possible, and ribbed with realistic veins. In length and girth it matched Alex's almost exactly, which was what I'd wanted. My desire was for him to experience what I get to feel every night.

But cross-dressing can also be a way to slide into a role. Not only to slip into someone else's knickers, but to be someone else. In my short story "Like a Girl," Ivy attempts to really be a boy for her lover:

"You're going to come for me, boy?" Logan murmured, crooning to me, but teasing somehow. Taunting me for dressing like this in the first place. He'd told me to buy an outfit for Cal. He hadn't told me to dress up myself.

"Yes, Sir."

"Then come."

My knees would have buckled if Logan hadn't used one hand to pin my shoulder against the wall, holding me in place easily as the shudders worked through me. The orgasm was almost frighteningly intense. Embarrassingly so, as I was being watched fiercely by the two men in my life. And then it was over, and Logan let me go, and I hiked up my jeans and sank down to the floor, letting the wall support me now.

"You even come like a girl," Logan said, as he poured himself a fresh drink.

In K. Lynn's "Undercover," the pleasure of panties is fully discovered:

"I've been waiting all day to do this," David said, looking at his boyfriend laid out on the bed. Keith was still fully clothed, waiting for David to undress him. "Couldn't stop thinking about you wearing them."

"Yeah?" Keith asked, his voice low and smooth. "Did it make you hard?"

"Couldn't you tell?" David asked, crawling up the mattress until he was poised over Keith's thighs. He straddled them, then sat up so that his hands could be free to work. "Every time you passed by me at the office, I was imagining what was underneath. Let's see if I guessed the color right."

David unbuttoned Keith's pants, taking care as he unzipped them to reveal the silky pink material beneath. Keith's dick was hard in the panties he wore, bulging out against the material as if he was going to break free any moment. David couldn't suppress the hot want that ran through him at the sight.

"So fucking beautiful like this," he said, leaning down to place a kiss against Keith's silk-covered dick. Keith rose up the contact, letting out a shuddering breath. "Love it, love you."

"They've been driving me crazy all day, too," Keith said, grunting as David mouthed his erection through the panties. "Rubbing against me,

cradling me. Thought I was going to come in my pants like some teenager."

"But you didn't," David said. *"And now I get to see you fall apart under me. Best present ever."*

Kat Watson writes in her story "Deborah":

I'd done as instructed—I was waxed completely bare, my legs and underarms were shaved.

Once I'd powdered the latex, I slipped the short dress over my head and prayed. To whom, I wasn't sure; I just needed someone to get me through this. Someone to help me find my strength to finally go through with what I'd fantasized about for years. Decades.

The snapping sound of the rubber contrasted with the smooth feel of it against my skin, and I sighed with mounting pleasure. The way it felt, the way it smelled, everything about it sang to me. The same way he sang to me.

When I was certain I'd tucked enough and at just the right angle, nothing tentatively falling out of the snug rubber briefs I had on, I put on the heels, grateful he'd chosen a modest height. I was unfamiliar with walking in them, and pushing six-foot-three anyway. No way he'd want me to tower over him.

"Are you ready to be shown off, Deborah?"

Hearing my name—my for-the-night name—from him sent tingles up my spine and made my dick snap further to attention.

"Yes, Sir."

Giselle Renarde understands how sexy cross-dressing can be, even solo, as she shows in this story called "Max Alone in See-Through Panties":

Not all Max's panties were pink, but most were. Various shades—hot pink, baby pink, some rosy, almost red. These ones were blush, like wine. They were mesh, a fine almost glossy fabric, and sheer enough that if you caught them at the right angle you could see straight through.

Max didn't always spend this much time staring in the mirror. He wore women's panties every day now. His little treat. He deserved to feel good, so why not? It was rare that he used the urinal at work—he'd never been a fan. He preferred to pee in private.

Besides, he didn't need everyone getting in his business. Secrets were secret for a reason. It's not that he felt ashamed. Well, okay, maybe he felt a little ashamed, but not as much as he used to. Panties were part of life now. Sure they were his favorite part of any outfit, but they were still just clothing. It's not like they were sex.

Which is not to say that panties didn't make him think about sex. Every time he slipped into a fresh pair and felt that sheer lightweight fabric against the sensitive flesh of his balls, a hot shudder ran through him. When he pulled on a pair of panties and the elastic material snapped against his dick, it always hardened just a bit. And sometimes more than a bit.

And sometimes a lot more.

"Packing Heat," by K. Lynn, shows that it doesn't take much effort to make a change that will transform your sex life:

After five years together, Sandy didn't think there was anything her girlfriend could do that would surprise her, but she should learn to stop making assumptions.

"Having fun?" Rebecca asked as she walked up. She didn't try to change her voice, or appear to be trying to pass completely. Here she stood in a white men's dress shirt and black pants, her short hair slicked back like one of those 1930s movie gangsters they were so fond of watching.

"What's all this?"

"Costume party, right? Figured I'd try out the other side for a night."

"As long as you're not trying it out with anyone but me," Sandy said, closing the distance between them. She ran her hands along her girlfriend's chest, feeling the binding underneath the shirt. "Damn, how much wrapping did you have to do to get those things to stay down?"

"Lots. Can't hardly breathe," Rebecca said, placing her hands on each

side of Sandy's cheeks and diving in for a kiss. "But you look nice in your fairy costume."

"Grant you a wish?"

"Actually, I was thinking I might provide that," Rebecca said, pushing her crotch against Sandy's.

When she did, Sandy felt a bulge that definitely did not belong. Her eyes widened at the contact, her body pressing against the hardness. "You're packing?"

"Figured we might have a little fun later," Rebecca said, kissing her girlfriend again.

"Or now," Sandy said, arching up into her. "I vote now."

I vote now, too. Because whether you're a boy dressing as a girl, a girl as a boy—or something in between—playing with a brand-new-to-you wardrobe can be an enlightening, exotic experience.

TANTALIZING TIPS

- Haunt thrift stores for starters. A complete transformation doesn't have to empty your wallet. Plus, you might get ideas from perusing racks of vintage clothing.

- Plan an evening in which you and your partner dress head-to-toe as the opposite sex. No peeking until the big reveal. See where this saucy scenario leads.

- Venture out in public while dressed in drag. Halloween is often a safe way to try this for the first time. But you don't have to save the fun for once a year. Host a costume party if you don't want to take the show on the road.

TANGLED UP IN BLUE

SOPHIA VALENTI

When I found the panties, I'll admit that I immediately thought the worst. I had been putting away the laundry when I noticed the neatly folded satin nestled between Chad's no-nonsense cotton briefs. I knew right away they weren't mine; blue was never my color.

My heart fell as I picked up the panties, already trying to imagine the woman to whom they belonged. But I was also confused. Chad and I worked from home and were practically inseparable. Never mind motive or desire—when could he possibly find the time to cheat?

I held the lace-trimmed garment by the waistband, with a million thoughts running through my mind. One of which was: *That's why he always insists on putting away his own clothes!* I wondered what other drawers he had in his drawer.

My dismay was just about to take a sharp turn toward anger, when Chad interrupted my reverie. "They're mine," he said, his voice quavering.

"What do you mean?" I spun around to face him, not knowing what the hell he was talking about. He was looking sheepish, and he was blushing to the roots of his dark blond hair.

"The panties. They're mine," he stammered. "I-I like to wear them sometimes."

The embarrassment on his face was undeniable, and I knew right away that he was telling me the truth. At first I was so relieved he wasn't sleeping with another woman that the full effect of his words didn't register. But a heartbeat later, when the silence between us seemed charged with increasing tension, I realized he needed a response from me other than a wide-eyed stare.

"You like to wear panties." I repeated the words, buying myself a little more time. But as I spoke, I could already picture him in my head: tall and muscular, satin and lace—an intriguing combination. And the more I thought about it, the more I wanted to see him draped in that beautiful blue satin.

Chad nodded, his tongue darting out to lick his lips nervously. I could see the worry clouding his blue-green eyes—eyes that nearly matched his knickers. I knew that sharing this secret was huge. It was bigger than us moving in together, and even bigger than getting married. It was easy for him to say he loved me. It was far more difficult to admit that he loved panties.

"Show me," I whispered, offering him the slippery bit of satin. My voice cracked, my nerves finally catching up with his. This was uncharted territory for me, but my desire seemed to have me acting on autopilot. Chad reached out, taking my hand in his as we held the garment between us. His fingers brushed against my palm through the delicate fabric, that gentle touch sending shivers down my spine. We kept our hands locked together for a moment, with the panties crushed between our fingers. Looking deep into his eyes, I knew that everything was going to be okay. This kink of his was a minor detour in our journey together, but it was an enticing adventure that I wanted to take with him.

Chad pulled away, taking the panties from me and beginning to strip. His days of college football were long behind him, but he still had the body of an athlete. I admired every bit of masculine flesh as it was revealed, seeing his muscles grow taut as he reached up to pull his T-shirt over his head. His hair was now mussed, but he didn't make a move to fix it. Instead, he picked up the pace and shucked off his jeans and briefs. His cock was already semirigid, and I had to stop myself from reaching out to stroke him. I was already aching for him, but I wanted the picture in my head to become reality. I wanted to see him wearing those panties, and I wanted to stroke his cock through that shiny satin.

Once Chad was naked, he held the panties in front of him, ready to step into the delicate underwear. However, he waited a beat, as if giving me a moment to back out, but that wasn't going to happen. I felt like I was seeing my husband for the very first time, with his lust finally laid as bare as his flesh.

"Do it," I whispered, surprised by how husky my voice sounded.

Chad bit his lip and then took a deep breath that he released as he slipped first one leg and then the other into the panties. As he slowly pulled them upward, I moved closer, my hands joining his at the waistband. He released his grip, smiling shyly as I raised the panties up over his thighs. I had to smile, too, when I needed to pull the satin out and up in order to cover his erect cock, which was now as hard as I'd ever seen it. Slipping my fingers just underneath the waistband, I smoothed out the wide strip of elasticized lace, running my thumbs along the outside as a guide.

Despite the very unladylike bulge in the front, the panties fit him like a dream. Not too big and not too small. Chad didn't know what I expected of him, so he simply stood still and quiet as I absorbed my first vision of him in his precious panties. He was a sight to behold, with his stubble-covered chin and disheveled hair, and broad shoulders that tapered to a trim waist. My eyes traveled down his flat stomach, lingering at his well-defined muscles before settling on the sleek satin that spanned his hips and barely covered the evidence of his arousal. It was fascinating to me that a simple piece of fabric could carry so much weight and worry—and inspire so much passion and lust.

I let my fingers play at his lacy waistband, while I walked around his body. Caressing him as I moved, I felt his abs quiver under my fingertips, which I continued to slide around his waist before running them over the taut cheeks of his ass.

Without a word, I slipped my arms around him, embracing him from behind. The back panel of his panties felt slippery as I ground my body against his, letting my hands roam over his pecs. I kept the fingers of one hand splayed across his chest, stroking the smattering of hair there, as I moved the other hand downward. As I gently brushed his erection, Chad uttered a soft moan and its sexy vibrations resonated within my own body, making my nipples peak and my pussy moisten. I let my fingers play over his bulge, sightlessly savoring the contrast of his steely erection swathed in such feminine fabric. The satin hugged every ridge in his shaft, and although I had touched, kissed and licked his cock countless times, this familiar terrain suddenly felt exciting and new.

Chad turned in the circle of my arms. I was still completely dressed, but he quickly took care of that. Losing his shyness, he reverted to the take-charge guy I was used to, and within a matter of minutes, the only thing between us was that magical scrap of blue. Leaning down, my husband held my head in place by weaving his fingers through my long, dark hair so he could kiss me deeply. I closed my eyes, surrendering to him as I shamelessly rubbed my body against his. I loved the feeling of the satin against my bare flesh, and I loved even more that every one of my movements made the panties stroke Chad's erection and caused him to groan against my lips.

When we finally broke apart, Chad's face was flushed and he was gazing at me with eyes half-lidded with lust. I backed him toward the bed, not even bothering to clear away the unfolded laundry that was still piled there. With stray thongs and mismatched socks surrounding him, Chad settled back and I knelt between his spread thighs.

Chad looked down at me, the erratic rise and fall of his chest betraying the fragile state of his control. I caressed the front of his panties once more, tugging the fabric taut and witnessing up close what my fingers had already observed: Chad's cock was impressively erect and straining mightily against the front of his dainty undergarment. I stroked the length of his pole, which made him thrust his hips upward aggressively as he tried to increase the pressure of my touch. Tossing my hair to one side, I lowered my head and took a long, slow lick of his shaft.

"Oh, baby, that's sweet," he uttered in a fractured whisper.

My tongue easily glided along the satin, so I kept repeating the motion, enjoying the way the wet fabric darkened and clung to his erection, covering him like a second skin. I liked teasing him this way, but it was getting harder and harder to ignore the frantic pulsations of my own sex. This drawn-out play—from Chad's striptease and fashion show to his passionate kisses—had made my pussy throb with desire. I could feel the evidence of my arousal dampening my thighs.

I rocked backward on my heels, squeezing my legs together to give myself some relief, but the action only made me more desperate for him. But before I fully surrendered to my lust, I wanted Chad to tell me more—to reveal all of his satin-filled fantasies.

"Tell me why you like them, Chad. I want to know." I continued to stroke his cock, coaxing out little spasms of pleasure.

"I like the way they feel against my skin, the way the material is so cool and slippery. It's not rough and boring like cotton, and it looks so…"

"Pretty?"

"Yes…pretty," he answered, breathless.

Now he was blushing fire-engine red. From his response, I could tell that wearing panties involved more than appreciating the tactile sensation of fabric. There was another dream lurking within him. One I wanted to make come true. Why? Because I love him, and bringing him joy brings me joy, too.

"I can help you."

"With what?"

"To be pretty." I leaned down once more, taking another leisurely lick of the front of his panties. The head of his cock was now peeking out of the top of the waistband, and I fluttered the tip of my tongue against the underside of it.

"Oh, yes," he hissed, balling some of the stray laundry in his fists.

I cupped Chad's sac through the satin, stroking my thumb along his most sensitive spots, knowing that the sensations would be amplified by the fabric commanding his erotic attention. I nudged down the waistband of the panties and wrapped my fingers around his cock, jerking him ever so slowly.

"I want to dress you up," I confessed, surrendering my secrets the moment the pictures formed in my mind. "Buy you pretty lingerie, and make love to you while you're dressed head-to-toe like a beautiful lady. *My* beautiful lady."

Chad's face was a vision of helpless ecstasy. He'd gotten lost in the scene I'd painted with my words. I could tell that he was fervently hoping I wasn't teasing. He raised his hips, wishing and reaching with every fiber of his being for the fulfillment of his long-held fantasies.

I grabbed the sides of his panties and pulled them down just enough to free his hard cock. Holding his shaft steady, I swooped down to take the entire length of him in my mouth. Chad groaned, grabbing my hair as I deep-throated him. I held him in place for a few seconds, before pulling away.

"Kiss me, baby," he murmured in a needy whisper as he grabbed me and took me into his arms. With his cock pressed between our writhing bodies, I lowered my lips to his. Chad kissed me wildly, as if he was on the verge of losing complete control. I wasn't far behind him, so I reached down to take hold of his dick and position it at the entrance of my pussy. One day I would take the time to drape him in silks and satins, but not today. My hunger for him had grown too strong to ignore; I needed to feel him inside me.

Breaking our lip-lock, I sat up and then lowered myself onto his shaft, sighing loudly as he stretched and filled me. Once I'd hit bottom, I snugged my knees up against his hips—and the panties that were still banded around his thighs. The sensation of the crumpled satin sparked my sexual imagination again, and my mind began to conjure up scenarios for the two of us.

"You'll let me, won't you? You'll let me make you my pretty girl?" This time I was the one who was begging. I cupped Chad's face with my hand, running my thumb across his quivering bottom lip that I could already imagine slicked with ruby-red. I wanted to kiss him with my own gloss-covered lips, and the strength of that desire was such a sexy surprise. What had started out as Chad's secret kink had woven itself into my libido. His passion had become my own, my lust irrevocably entwined with his.

"Yes," he answered, pumping his hips upward and making his dick hit the sweetest spots inside me. I rocked my body forward to snatch another moment of pure pleasure. Despite his frilly fantasies, I was glad he was still a man—in that he had a hard cock to satisfy me. Rhythmically riding his shaft, I reached back between Chad's thighs to stroke him through the satin—fingering his constricted sac and wriggling my fingers even lower to tease the sensitive patch of flesh above his asshole. Massaging him there caused Chad to release a feral growl, and he bucked upward, driving his dick in me to the hilt and leaving me momentarily breathless.

Chad met my downward thrusts with forceful movements of his own, crushing my clit against the base of his cock every time we connected. Our frenzied movements had settled into a hard and fast rhythm that was rapidly taking us higher and higher. My husband took hold of my hips, in order to drive into me more intensely. I lost some of my control as I quivered atop him. Leaning back, I grabbed the sides of his panties to hold myself steady. I closed my eyes as I recalled how he looked, standing in front of me in those blue undies. Keeping that picture in my mind's eye, I savored the sensation of Chad's cock slamming up into me and sparking my climax. As I cried out, I yanked at the satin, pulling it more tightly against Chad's body and making him groan as he came inside me.

I collapsed atop him, knowing that the panties were a damp, tangled mess, which only meant he'd need more—and I knew just where to get them.

CHAPTER TWELVE

TWIST ME, TAUNT ME, TURN ME ON—
FETISHES

"Wow, three pairs of shoes! Someone had a fetish."
—MARGE SIMPSON

You'd be hard pressed to find a fetish I don't have an affinity for. In fact, I probably have a fetish for being hard pressed. I love the standard choices on the menu—high heels, stockings, feathers, tickling, boots, lace, leather, nylons, fishnets, piercing, lipstick, ponytails… And yes, I know all about your more unusual fetishes—shrimping, sploshing, plushies, looners.

Fetishes can definitely have a place in your world. Whether you're into animate fetishes (fingers, feet, breasts, legs…) or inanimate (all those lovely, lovely items you can dress up in or rub up against), fetishes are a simple way to broaden your kinky horizon.

Many fetishes are free (it costs nothing to lust after a beautiful pair of feet) or fairly inexpensive. Have a thing for stockings? Nylons are easy to buy—even at a grocery store. And how sexy is that? You and your partner knowing that those stockings aren't for work, they're for play.

My story "Not for Sale" features two stocking-fetishists:

"Closer," he said, "I want to touch the merchandise."

Her feet moved forward without any instruction from her brain. She felt hypnotized. When she had gotten close enough, he stroked his hands up her nylon-clad legs, and then palmed the flesh of her thighs where the stockings ended, touching bare skin with bare skin. His hands were warm and big. She wanted him to place his entire palm over her pussy, to let her rest her snatch against him. She wanted him to part her pussy lips and drag the tips of his fingers between them, touching, just barely touching, her clit.

He did none of those things. He simply stayed still, with his palms on her thighs, and waited for her to continue.

Rhiannon sucked in her breath. He didn't know her secret. Not yet. But he would soon. What would happen if Sara needed something from the back room? What would happen if the owner made a spot inspection and pounded on the stockroom door? What would happen if this stranger suddenly lifted her dress all the way up and saw her naked pussy? This is what did happen, the best of the possible scenarios coming true.

"I knew you weren't wearing panties."

"Rubbernecking" is my love letter to those who worship rubber. All that's required is a pair of rubber gloves. Gloves are one of those items you can purchase at hardware stores or five-and-dimes that will raise no eyebrows, but will definitely tent a pair of slacks. I do love buying kinky things when nobody is the wiser:

Once on the bed, I could slow down once more, reach for the box hidden in my nightstand drawer. A shake of cornstarch from a bottle by my lamp would help those thin white rubber gloves slide on smoothly, but I would take my time anyway. Making sure to smooth out any wrinkles, growing wetter with the caress of the rubber around each fingertip. When the gloves were on fully, I would interlace my fingers, watching the rubber meet rubber.

Now, it would become more difficult to go slowly. With hands that were like someone else's, some stranger's, I would touch myself while I recreated the window displays in my mind. Fingers gliding over my breasts, I imaged the window dresser—with his long dark hair, slim body—dressing me in the pale orange rubber sheath he'd slid on a mannequin the week before. Or slipping me into sleek scarlet rubber boots that would reach past my knees. I could see him buckling that bright red ball gag into place between my own parted lips, knowing somehow what that sensation would be like, what I would look like, gagged like that.

Snag a used plaid skirt at a thrift store, and you're halfway to the sex scene I penned in "Want"—you only need two kinky roommates to complete the vision:

Vincent had Lia over his lap, and he was punishing her sweet, sassy ass with a paddle. I'd seen that ass swish down the hallway. I had seen it when she'd bent over to unload the laundry. Seen it when she went prancing out the door in a far-too-short, schoolgirl skirt, which I now saw was in a crumpled ball on the floor. But this was my favorite time. Because he was wielding that paddle with finesse, and Lia continued to cry out and kick her heels and pound her fists uselessly in protest. Or mock protest. I wondered if she could have gotten free if she had tried hard enough. But then I saw Vincent grimace and grab both of her hands in one of his. He pinned her wrists neatly at the small of her back and then let go a volley of blows on her hindquarters.

Andrea Dale waxes rhapsodic about feet in "A Sensitive Sole":

The first time I found out just how sensitive her feet were—and how she reacted to sole stimulation, we were on the sofa, watching TV. She was lying with her feet in my lap, wearing just a simple pair of flat, slip-on sandals, the kind with nothing more than a jeweled strap between the toes to hold them on.

She'd had a long day, and I'm a nice girl, so I took off one of the sandals, intending to give her a foot massage.

She looked up, startled. "Oh, no, Katie. I—"

Her words degenerated into a groan when I pressed my thumbs gently into the ball of her right foot. I knew many people were ticklish, and I've been told I do a stellar job of massaging feet without causing undue tickling.

It was only after a moment or two of kneading that I realized Maya's groans were not just ones that came from major enjoyment of a great foot massage.

Her nipples were diamond hard and drilling their way through her thin cotton T-shirt.

Well, wasn't that interesting? I ran one hand along her leg from shapely calf to smooth thigh, and higher, under the short, flippy skirt she wore.

Her panties were, not to put too heavy a point on it, soaked.

As tempting as it was to just dive in and savor the feast before me, I was curious to see how far this fetish of hers went, just how excited I could get her.

I could fill an entire book with fetish stories. (Oh, wait. I have: *F Is for Fetish*.) Truly, they are unending. Addicting. Explore your own. Dig deep down into what gives you pleasure. And share the experience with your partner. Who knows? You might find a few more fetishes up your sleeve, or down your garter, that you didn't even know you had.

TANTALIZING TIPS

- Where there's a need for a how-to, you'll find Violet Blue. Her *Fetish Sex: An Erotic Guide for Couples* is sure to answer the questions of any curious fetishers-to-be.

- Some fetishes are easy to accessorize—such as wearing rubber gloves or donning a corset. However, others take a bit more planning. Don't let that stop you! If sploshing is on your menu, set aside enough time to make or purchase the foods, stretch out plastic sheeting, and indulge.

- Host your own Fetish Fridays. Visit a different fetish each week. Try nylons one week, knickers the next. If you find a fetish that floats your boat, slide it into a regular rotation.

THE SILK ROAD

DONNA GEORGE STOREY

I'm standing at the kitchen sink, rinsing off the last of the dinner dishes, when Julian comes up behind me and wraps his arms around my waist.

"Do you want to wear your silk stockings tonight?" he whispers.

My whole body stiffens.

"You do, don't you?"

It's not really a question.

"Y...yes," I stutter, my throat suddenly as dry as the Mongolian steppe.

"Be ready then," he says, and slips away. A few moments later, I hear him in the dining room, helping our older son with his algebra homework.

My hands go through the motions of loading the dishwasher, but my face feels hot, my pussy tingles and my mind is already busy planning for tonight's journey on the Silk Road. That's how I like to see it:

an endless length of translucent silk, fluttering over craggy mountain passes, across golden deserts, through cities ruled by turbaned tyrants. And just as the real Silk Road beguiled travelers with perfumes, fine carpets, spices and jewels, we, too, will visit strange lands and enjoy exotic pleasures.

On ordinary nights, I use the evening hours to wind down, relax and prepare for refreshing sleep. But my husband's simple whispered words mean this is no ordinary night. Already my senses are on high alert. When Julian sits next to me on the sofa, I'm keenly aware of the scent of him, a masculine fragrance of leather and cumin and sun-toasted grain. I glance up at his face and he smiles, his eyes sparkling like emeralds.

He's thinking of the Silk Road, too.

Finally, it's time to kiss the kids good night and settle them snugly in their respective bedrooms. Julian changes into his bathrobe and mumbles that he has a few emails to take care of in his office. With a knowing look, he leaves me alone in our bedroom to make the necessary preparations.

My pulse quickening, I pull open the top drawer of my dresser and snake my hand behind the control-top panty hose to my secret stash of lingerie. I carefully pull out a package of opalescent silk stockings. Placing it on the hope chest at the bottom of our bed, I head for the closet and take my white marabou mules from their shoebox. The five-inch heels are so slender, I can barely stand in them, much less walk more than a few steps. But the Silk Road is not for walking. I set the sexy slippers next to the stockings.

Then I undress and put on my Japanese kimono, knotting the belt loosely. A moment later, I hear a faint knock at the door. Julian has the timing down just right. Not wanting to raise my voice, I hurry to let him in. He flips the lock behind him with a metallic click that resonates deep inside me.

Julian glances over at the stockings and high heels, then back at me, a faint smile playing at his lips. He gives me a deep, knee-melting kiss.

And so the journey begins.

When our lips finally part, Julian takes my hand and guides me over to our bed. As I watch, he peels back the blankets and arranges our two pillows at the center of the headboard, as if readying the place for a pampered guest.

Who, of course, is none other than myself.

Julian settles me on the bed then gestures to the belt of my robe. "May I?"

I nod, suddenly too shy to speak.

He unties the belt and pulls my robe open, arranging the flaps around me. It's an odd, and exciting, effect—to lie totally nude on my outspread garment like a virgin sacrifice. Julian gives me a final once-over then picks up the package of stockings and lounges on the bed at my feet, one knee bent, the other leg stretched toward me. I have to admit he looks a bit like a sultan, especially with his robe falling open over his strong chest.

"May I put on the stockings now?"

His tone is respectful, even subservient, and yet that simple question makes my body feel weightless, lifted up out of time and completely subject to his whim.

"Yes, please," I say softly.

He slides one stocking from the package but pauses, rubbing the silk gently between his fingers. "I'm always amazed by these things. They feel so cool and light. Like a whisper."

"They feel good on my legs, too." I smile.

Julian lifts his eyebrows. "I wonder if they'd feel good on other places, too?"

I feel a flutter between my legs. "What other places did you have in mind?"

"Close your eyes and you'll find out."

I fight my natural urge to resist, mainly because Julian's naughty little detours have never disappointed me. So I obediently close my eyes, aware of my quick, shallow breath and the prickle of expectation on my naked skin. I gasp at the first touch of silk sweeping over my belly. The sensation is cool and impossibly subtle, yet it stimulates my nerves in the most beguiling way. I arch up and sigh. Humming approval, Julian trails the end of the stocking in sinuous shapes over my rib cage then circles my breasts, finally teasing each nipple to a hard point with a silk stocking pendulum. By now I'm struggling to keep my composure.

"Feel nice?" Julian asks, rather gratuitously.

"Yes."

"I could do this all night, but your bare legs are looking jealous. Keep your eyes closed. I'll tell you when to open them."

I love to watch him sheathe my legs in the luxurious silk stockings, but blindness brings unforeseen pleasures. I'm exquisitely aware of his warm fingers easing the bunched stocking over my toes, then rolling them up over my ankle all the way to my upper thigh, just a few short—and yet excruciatingly distant—inches from my swollen cleft.

"They do feel nice on your legs, don't they?" He runs his hand over the silk. "One more to go."

And so he repeats the process at the same ceremonial pace.

"There's something so erotic about this, when you're wearing nothing but stockings. They frame your...charms...so perfectly. See for yourself."

Suddenly self-conscious, I reluctantly open my eyes. But Julian is right. There is something particularly wanton about the vision of my white thighs and exposed mons, lush with auburn curls, floating above the virginal stockings.

"Look how your legs shimmer. The limbs of a goddess."

My long, slim legs have always gotten me compliments, but Julian's appreciation is as close as I've gotten to sheer worship. Over the years, I've grown to like it very much indeed.

"Would you like a foot massage? To help you relax?" Julian's smile is the perfect blend of deference and mischief. We both know his "massage" is likely to have quite the opposite effect.

Without waiting for a reply, he wraps his large, warm hand around my right foot and begins to probe the tight spots along the arch with his thumb. Julian's studied up on reflexology—very fitting given his proclivities—and at first his technique does lull me into a dreamy state. Stretched out indolently on the bed, a memory floats into my head, of a Chinese film we saw years ago. It was about a wealthy man with four wives. The wife chosen for his amorous attentions each night was honored with a red lantern at her door and a special foot massage, because the jaded master believed it helped a woman "better serve her man." The movie was darkly claustrophobic and had a tragic ending, and yet when Julian and I got home from the theater, we went straight to bed and made love. Soon after that, he offered to massage my feet before we had sex—with a surprising, but much happier, ending.

Julian now pulls my left foot onto his lap.

I tense up instinctively.

Julian clicks his tongue. "Relax, darling. I just want to make you feel good."

Is there such a thing as "too good"?

He starts in on the ball of my foot, circling firmly over the flesh with the pad of his thumb. This is, in itself, harmless, but my body knows what's coming. When his fingers move to my arch to knead the tight muscle along the edge of my foot, a jolt of pleasure shoots straight to my groin. My vagina reflexively pushes out. A gush of arousal trickles down onto my robe.

I moan, half in shame, half in delight.

"Enjoying this?" he asks.

Not that I can answer with Julian stimulating my sweet spot so mercilessly. Through the veil of my lashes, I notice that my chest is flushed with a rosy sex rash and my nipples are as hard as pebbles. A fiery rope of pleasure twists from his fingers up along my inner leg to feed the throbbing knot deep in my cunt.

"Still works like a charm, doesn't it?"

"Please stop now. I might come, and I want you inside me." Desperate in my need, I brush my foot over his crotch. He's rock hard and probably has been for some time.

Julian chuckles and shifts away. "Patience. First we need to put on your magic slippers." He reaches for the marabou mules and slides them carefully onto my feet.

This new stimulation is less dangerous, but equally cunning. Julian once observed that the slippers mold my feet into the same strained position they assume when I have an orgasm. Indeed when I press my foot against the unnaturally steep curve of the sole, my pussy aches in anticipation. Sometimes Julian makes love to me as soon as the slippers are in place, but I can never be sure which route we'll take on any given night. This time, to my surprise, he deftly slips off the bed and kneels at my feet.

"The slippers make your legs look so feminine and elegant. Like a dream. I'm almost afraid to touch you now."

I take my cue and sit a little higher against the pillows. "What about your lips? You could show your appreciation by kissing the stockings from toe to top."

His eyes flicker.

"But no slobbering," I add regally. "These are expensive."

"Yes, I'll be careful." His voice is hoarse, slightly winded. As if in a trance, he takes my foot and presses his lips to my toes, then the arch, then the ankle.

I tilt my head back and focus on his soft mouth moving slowly but inexorably up my leg. Soon he has to crawl back up on the bed on all fours, his head lowered as if kowtowing to my heavenly legs. The adoration fills me with a heady rush of power. Am I really so enchanting I can bring a man to his knees?

When he reaches the top of the stockings, Julian pauses. I feel his hot breath against my thigh. A question hovers in the air between us.

"You may proceed," I say.

Exhaling in a grateful sigh, Julian's lips cross the border from silk to bare flesh. In this earthier realm, the rules apparently change. His kisses grow wetter until he's shamelessly caressing my naked thighs with his tongue. I pull my knees up and open, thinking, perversely, of the gate of a monumental temple on the banks of the Nile. Julian positions himself at the entrance to my "pink satin palace"—as he likes to call it on our Silk Road travels. He places a few decorous kisses of greeting on my nether lips. Then his tongue darts out and flicks my clitoris.

I clutch the top of the pillows, opening myself farther to him. My husband flirts with the sensitive nub of flesh, but soon he is lashing it greedily until I'm squirming and juicing all over his face.

"Do it, goddamn it, fuck me," I growl.

"As my lady commands," he whispers. Then he's up on his knees, pulling open his robe to reveal a very impressive erection. My mouth is watering, I want it so bad, but he teases me, probing my entrance with his cock then pulling back to rub the wet knob over my clit. I return the favor by clenching my cunt muscles then pushing them open so quickly his cockhead is sucked into the hole. He gasps, then yields, sliding all the way in to the root.

We rest for a moment, gazing into each other's eyes.

"Stroke the stockings," I say. "Stroke the stockings while you fuck me."

With a grunt of assent, he pushes my knee up so my slippered foot dangles in midair. At the same time he begins to thrust slowly, deliberately. My inner walls are so inflamed from the extended foreplay, they thrill in the steady friction, up and down, up and down. I grip the pillow and point my toe, readying myself for arrival at our final destination.

When his fingers brush the top of my stocking, I cry out. Sparks shoot straight to my pussy, and my belly pulses with white heat. I thrust back, grinding my mons into his coarse pubic hair. Now we're struggling together, up a tall mountain, both of us lathered with sweat and female juice. Somehow he manages to keep caressing my thigh through the silk, tickling, teasing, taunting the sensitive nerves that are linked, by some mysterious sorcery, to my grasping cunt. Still we climb and climb, higher with each stroke, until suddenly my body is lifted into the air as if by a huge hand. And then just as suddenly I'm falling, hurtling through space, jerking and thrashing as I come. Julian rides my climax with me. With a few more deep strokes, he shoots inside me with a full-body shudder.

The trip isn't quite over yet, although the last part is easy, like floating on a river through a golden mist. I kick off the high heels and twine my silken legs around him while we glide with the current back to our ordinary life. There the landscape is gentle, even and pleasantly predictable—at least until our next adventure.

Because our passage to the Silk Road lies just inside my dresser drawer.

CHAPTER THIRTEEN

MORE THE MERRIER—
MÉNAGE

If two wrongs don't make a right, try three.

—LAURENCE J. PETER

Ménages have managed to make their way into popular culture. Mainstream ads for everything from liquor to margarine to plumbing devices feature potential ménage à trois. The idea of being sandwiched between two partners is a fantasy I've heard many times—and experienced, as well. (This is why I was thrilled to edit the book *Three-Way!*) What I adore about ménages is the constantly changing points of view. One person is the focal point, and then another, and then…yes, another. There is no back and forth. There's only round and round. And what's sexier than a circle?

Well, figuring out the logistics. That can be seriously sexy, as well.

In "Mercury in Retrograde," I write about an F/F/M situation:

I couldn't believe how matter-of-fact the couple was acting. I'd just been tongued and finger-fucked by Cynthia, had gone down on her in the shower, and now her man was stripping down and joining us beneath the spray. Was I the only one who found the situation unusual?

I stood, in a pathetic attempt to be a gracious hostess. Hello, Joe. Welcome to my shower. The thought made me giggle nervously, and Cynthia put her arms around my waist, as if to calm me down.

Joe had other plans. He slid in between us and got his mouth against my neck. "I've wanted to do this for so long," he said, before gently biting my skin. I could feel the arousal building inside me once more—or maybe it never had completely died down since my oily orgasm on the kitchen floor. "Cynthia and I both have."

"Why'd you wait so long?" I asked, turning to face him. The spray from the showerhead made us all wet, all over. The water droplets lingered on Joe's long dark eyelashes.

"You never want to overstep your boundaries," he said.

Kat Watson describes a couple on the make in her sexy story, "They Should Have Sent a Poet":

I'd spotted her in a bar, all rich brown hair, curvy legs and pouty red lips; who could've overlooked her?

When I asked Derrick if we could take her home and he agreed, I almost let out a squeal. We'd talked for weeks about inviting another woman to our bed, but we didn't seem to fit in with the swinging crowd in our area.

Her name was Lily, and watching Derrick between her thighs made me want to write poetry to her cunt.

"See right here?" he asked, his pointed tongue skimming over her clit. "Gentle."

I mimicked what he'd done and was startled when she bucked into my mouth, needing more. I sucked and licked, taking her lips between mine and finally focusing my attention back on her clit.

"You're doing so good, baby. She's going to come any second."

Lily's hands tugged painfully at my hair, holding me to her pulsing pussy as she did, indeed, come.

In a move they'd seemingly silently planned, they maneuvered me onto my back. One of Lily's hands flicking and teasing a nipple, the other with several fingers buried deep before I could take a deep breath. From above my slit, she winked at my husband then moved faster.

Unlike my tentative licks and touches, hers were certain, sure. Practiced.

"Do you like the way she licks you, baby?"

Derrick's words sent me flying, just like he knew they would.

Elisa Sharone's ménage piece, "Our First Girl," also focuses on two girls and a boy:

Fingers sliding between her wet lips, the memory of the threesome tickled at the back of her mind. They'd always been monogamous and faithful, but in recent months their sexual boundaries had become fluid and what was once taboo now seemed like an adventure. She stretched her long limbs out across the bed and closed her eyes, letting the image take hold.

He's watching her, this beautiful slender girl with long auburn hair straddling my hips and teasing my breasts. Her lips and teeth graze my nipple, her face hidden behind a curtain of curls. I can feel her pussy slipping against my skin as she rolls her hips and grinds against me. I pull our unexpected lover to my chest, holding her tightly as a kiss plays between our lips.

Then his cock slides easily into my slick heat and he thrusts hard against us both. And suddenly we're moving together, him holding her hips as though he's fucking her from behind while I draw him inside. I'm lost in the scent of her, the feeling of him. And together they make me come, both of their names on my lips.

"Tripartite," by Georgia E. Jones, details the pleasure of two men and a woman (and also the pleasures of oral outdoors):

Adam sank to the ground, pulling me with him. I ran my hands across his belly before pulling down his trunks and putting my mouth on his cock. He made a strangled sound, and I sucked on him, hard, crouched between his thighs, not giving him a chance to adjust. Will lifted me to my knees, stripping off my bikini and touching me, spreading me open, nudging me with the head of his cock. He knew exactly how much sex I hadn't been having since the divorce. Then I was filled up, the hot, thick length of Will inside me and hard thrust of Adam's cock in my mouth. It was what I wanted, bone deep and mindless. I couldn't establish any sort of rhythm, clenching around Will and grinding back against him. He said something—the dark voice of a cautionary tale—and held my hips in broad-palmed hands and did it for me.

I sucked on Adam, licking him up and down, cupping his balls in one hand then taking him as deep as I could until he touched the back of my throat. Adam came first, crying out, his hands fisted in my hair. I swallowed and rested my face against his belly, feeling Will thrust harder and harder, my own pleasure rising toward orgasm, but it was going to take longer than he had, so I just tightened around him as hard as I could and held on until he came.

We lay in a warm heap of tangled limbs. I measured my breathing against theirs, first Will's, then Adam's.

Dilo Keith's ménage excerpt from *Make Mine to Go* explores an erotic M/M/M scenario:

They expeditiously had me up against the headboard, with my cuffs affixed to the rails instead of to each other, and pillows between my back and the metal. With no warning, Paul straddled me and shoved his cock in my mouth. I struggled to back away, as if an extra inch would actually help me take him. Maybe it did, or maybe Paul eased off a little. It was more of a face fucking than a blow job, leaving me with little to do except breathe and keep my throat relaxed. Perfect. I couldn't have been much harder, not without begging for release.

From the sounds and movement of the headboard, I figured out Paul was holding on, using it for leverage. I groaned at the image of that and of Justin there watching me. I envisioned strong thighs driving Paul's groin against me, my mouth stretched around him, and my arms held by leather, grateful that the camera was saving this for wanking to later. When Paul was getting close, Justin started jerking me off. He was doing himself, too, which was why the rhythm was a bit more like his, a little slower than I preferred. Not that the particular strokes mattered when two hot men had me at their mercy.

Are you interested in M/F/M—or F/M/F? Or some scramble of the M's and the F's as yet undecided? (Doesn't it sound as if we're discussing a particularly sexy spoonful of alphabet soup?) Play out with fantasies before you make the first move. Then puzzle those pieces together.

TANTALIZING TIPS

- Put on a racy movie and pretend the people onscreen are in the room with you. (Read my story "Counterpane" for more insight.)

- If you're not ready to invite an actual third into your bedroom, incorporate phone sex or Skype to break down the barrier.

- Ménages can be enjoyable in many different varieties. If m/f/f works for you one time, try m/f/m the next.

MARGARITA MAGIC

THOMAS S. ROCHE

When Brian returned from blending margaritas in the kitchen, Robyn and Eve were making out on the love seat. If this turn of events wasn't a hundred percent unexpected, it still came as a surprise, for at least one unusual reason. Eve was, it had always been supposed, very much a lesbian. Brian had lived in San Francisco long enough and had enough queer friends to know that getting with a straight girl was thought in the lesbian community to be a big, fat, juicy invitation to the kind of drama that Eve, it was said, detested. Wasn't it an even bigger, fatter, juicier invitation for a lesbian to get with a straight girl while her husband was in the kitchen making margaritas?

And wasn't it even more so not to stop—or even slow down—when he came back?

Okay, but Brian had to admit that there had been hints. Eve didn't have a girlfriend and clearly didn't want one. And there had been flirting even before there had been margaritas as a topic of discussion.

In fact, there had been *lots* of flirting. Brian liked that; his taste in women tended toward the punky, and Eve was *hot*. But Brian wasn't a cad; he hadn't already counted a threesome in the bag. He was basically just counting on margarita magic to help the flirting continue. He hadn't guessed that things might escalate into a make-out session on the love seat.

But for margarita magic to even work—that is to say, for it to take a reasonable lesbian and make her think a threesome with a straight couple is an awesome idea, it usually takes at least a sip. Brian hadn't even gotten Eve to taste the damn things, and here she was with his wife's tongue in her mouth. Sure, that sweet mescal enchantment didn't always need to cross the blood-brain barrier to work...but didn't it at least need to pass Eve's lips?

Apparently not before Robyn's tongue did.

Brian set his intoxicating pitcher of frothy green sex on the coffee table. He sat in the soft easy chair facing the big, cushy love seat that held his wife and their guest.

He poured himself a tall one.

He took a mouthful of cool sweet magic and settled in to watch. Neither woman paid a damned bit of attention to him, which suited Brian just fine for the moment.

Robyn was half-atop their guest, and the two women were going at it furiously—making out as if they couldn't get enough of each other. In fact, they were more than making out; Robyn's hand was well up Eve's dress, though there wasn't that much of the dress, really, for it to be "up." Among their friends and the friends of their friends, Eve was the famous femme slut in any given room, and tended to sometimes push her luck...her luck being the plausible deniability when she managed to flash anyone who would be scandalized but no one who would be pleasantly titillated. This dress was the sluttiest of the bunch, apparently sewn from an oversized Stooges T-shirt, short in the hem and so low cut she had practically been falling out of it all night. Its structural instability was augmented by a tactical series of hacks and slashes cut right through Iggy Pop's grotesque yet oddly compelling bod, as if the naked torso of Eve's addled idol was about to start bleeding on her. Admiring Eve in barely there punk clothes was so completely part and parcel of being her friend that when she'd shown up in this one, Brian hadn't considered it the obvious invitation that Robyn had. Hey, they were just a straight couple having dinner with their barely dressed lesbian friend and then inviting her back to their place to listen to some Tom Verlaine solo albums, right? Hey, what could be suggestive about that?

Brian slurped. Margarita Magic exploded in his mouth.

Robyn was all the way on top of Eve, now, their bodies pushed up together. Robyn pinned Eve's wrists down on the cushy arm of the love seat, with one palm flat across them. Her other hand was up under Iggy Pop's crotch and down Eve's panties, which were visible between Eve's wide-spread legs. They were pink, of all things, with red bows, sort of a see-through mesh, and they undulated as Robyn's fingers worked fervently. His wife was urgently finger-fucking their ' guest while her ravenous mouth made bestial sounds all up and down Eve's neck.

Eve was moaning, her hips rising and falling with the motions of Robyn's hand. Brian's cock began to stiffen, but only a little; he wanted to watch until someone invited him in. Why kill the goose that laid the golden threesome?

Robyn had magic fingers. Brian often kissed and sucked them; he loved to feel them digging sharp-nailed into his flesh. They weren't sharp-nailed now; Robyn had just had a manicure, which Brian realized in retrospect might have been another sign that his wife had been thinking something could happen tonight between the three of them—or at least between her and Eve. Now, one of Robyn's magic hands had both of Eve's wrists pinned. Eve didn't let this dissuade her from fully participating in her own ravishment. Eve's hips worked sensuously up and down against Robyn as she sought to fuck herself more firmly onto Robyn's other hand.

The two kissed hungrily; Robyn never stopped finger-fucking Eve. There was something desperate and urgent about the way they kissed. Brian's cock rose from half to full erection. He bit his lip, afraid that jumping in too soon might spoil everything.

Slowly, deliberately, Brian took a long deep slurp of margarita.

It wasn't easy for Brian to keep his distance. One of Robyn's perfect teacup-sized tits had popped out of her bra, showing a whisper of hot pink finger marks. Had Eve been pawing his girlfriend while he was making margaritas—before Robyn had pinned Eve's wrists? Now that was fucking hot; he hadn't been gone that long. They must have gotten busy almost the second he left. He had probably been barely out the door when Robyn and Eve surged together and made with the lip-lock...

Brian's eyes narrowed. Did that mean the pair didn't want him involved? Was he even—maybe—fucking things up by being here, watching?

Brian took a deep draught of margarita, never taking his eyes off the passionately kissing women.

He was still swallowing when Roby and Eve looked at him at once.

They started to laugh.

And then it was Eve who said in the practiced drawl of a forties film maven:

"What's the matter, big-boy, you just wanna watch?"

Brian opened his mouth to say something stupid about how he wasn't sure they wanted him joining in; he stopped himself barely in time. The two girls laughed and teased him. "He's blushing!" they said. Any other time, that would have irritated Brian and made him blush more, but he decided tonight Robyn and Eve deserved a whole lot of slack.

Brian got up, refilled his glass and approached the couch. Robyn, still laughing, reached up and plucked the drink from his hand; she planted those bee-stung lips on the straw and slurped up just enough margarita so that when she lunged back down to kiss Eve, the latter issued a purr, then a whimper as the cold hit her, then a giggle.

Brian barely even noticed that their guest's hand had found his belt and was grabbing and unfastening it.

With his belt as a handhold, Eve pulled Brian down *hard*. He dropped to his knees beside the love seat. Sticky margarita splashed and dribbled down Eve's neck, chased by Robyn's eager tongue. Brian felt Eve's hand unzipping his fly and tugging his jockeys out of the way. Her hand disappeared into Brian's pants and came out holding his erect cock.

By the time Eve got Brian's cock out, Robyn had Eve's dress up past her tits and was deftly undoing her bra. While Robyn was occupied with that, Eve took the margarita from Robyn's hand and sucked down a healthy slurp. Then she made *yum* sounds as she lunged for Brian's cock. She put her spit-wet lips on it, cool with margarita and sticky with kiss-ruined lipstick. Her mouth glided up and down the underside of Brian's erect cock, her tongue slipping out as she got her bearings. She licked all the way down to the base of Brian's shaft. Then she came back up to the top and engulfed his cock with her mouth.

Brian sighed softly as he felt Eve's mouth surrounding him, cool at first and then past the point where the sweet margarita had actively chilled her. Instead, as Eve pressed Brian's cockhead up against the back of her throat, he felt the chill of the blended ice and the easy warmth at the back of her mouth. Eve had a piercing through her tongue, and Brian could feel it against his *glans*, strangely stimulating and hot. Eve's mouth bobbed up and down while her eyes flickered up, the dark orbs smiling at Brian.

When she came up for air, she said: "You have *no* idea how much I miss these when I don't have one around."

Once again Brian opened his mouth and almost said something stupid ("You can visit this one whenever you want?" "This one misses you?" "They're not hard to find?") but managed to stop himself. Robyn had Eve's dress up to her shoulders and her bra was halfway off, but Eve didn't want to stop sucking his cock. She finally made a bratty little irritated gesture and put up her arms and sat up just enough so that Robyn could get the dress over Eve's head. The bra went, too, tangled up with it, until all that was left were the panties and the big heavy cyberpunk combat boots with the big metal buckles. And while the boots looked impressive on Eve's mostly nude body, the panties weren't much to speak of. Robyn tugged them out of the way with very little effort as she slid down Eve's body and started eating her out.

Eve moaned softly as she worked on Brian's cock, reaching around him to get his pants down over his ass, then down to his ankles. He kicked off his shoes and stepped out of them, going to a great deal of trouble to get his socks off as well—the last damned thing he wanted to do was have a threesome in *socks*. He made short work of his shirt while Eve went to town on his cock. Despite rumors of her only liking girls, Eve was clearly an expert at this. Her mouth worked up and down his cock eagerly, her tongue gliding easily over the underside of his shaft. Every once in a while, however, Robyn—whose face was still buried between Eve's tattooed thighs—would do something particularly delicious with her tongue, and Eve's mouth would come off Brian's cock. She would utter a noise of pleasure—whether a sibilant hiss or a soft, rolling moan—and launch herself into the task of sucking Brian's cock with newfound abandon.

And yet, she obviously knew what she was doing; she wasn't building Brian toward a climax. The way her mouth worked, she could have—but she was teasing him, stroking him, gently coaxing more pleasure out of him while Robyn kept working on her sex. Robyn was no longer licking Eve but was using her hand to fuck her silly.

In fact, Robyn—who didn't get to play with girls very often—was showing an abiding obsession with Eve's pussy. Her fingers had made their way deep inside her, and Brian could see Eve's smooth sex stretched tight around three—no, four—of Robyn's fingers, the ring through her clit glinting bewitchingly under Robyn's thumb. At some point—Brian couldn't be sure when—the panties had been slid over Eve's boots, leaving the punk girl nude except for those giant leather and metal monstrosities.

Eve worked her hips furiously, fucking herself onto Robyn's hand. Although Eve's own hand was still wrapped around the base of Brian's spit-wet cock, it became very clear very fast that Eve no longer had the concentration to give him a proper blow job. She was losing it, mounting closer to orgasm with each eager thrust of her body onto Robyn's hand—which made Eve's own hand tighten around Brian's cock as if it were a grab bar. Her cries of pleasure grew louder with each stroke. The expression on Robyn's face was priceless—the kind of bliss only possible in a married girl who wants very badly to play with other girls, and finally gets to.

Brian took it upon himself to extricate his cock from Eve's death grip and sneak his hands up under Robyn's arms. He got her shirt open quickly and worked on her bra; even when he started kissing her, Robyn would only let him slide one of her hands through the armhole and strap, because she wanted to keep fucking Eve. Her blouse and bra hung awkwardly from one shoulder while Robyn's fingers plunged deep into Eve. Robyn's skirt was much easier, because by then Robyn was half standing to get leverage, and Eve was very close to a climax.

But Robyn knew what she was doing with a pussy almost as much as Eve knew what she was doing with a cock, so she didn't rush forward and get Eve off quickly; she *toyed* with her, while her husband slid her clothes off.

By the time Robyn lunged forward onto Eve and leaned in hard to kiss her and fuck her harder, she was stark-raving naked. The two women lip-locked eagerly while Brian, winded from the wrestling match it took to get Robyn undressed, took a slurp of margarita—and to his surprise, got pulled in hard for a kiss, Eve's hand on the back of his head.

She kissed him hungrily while his mouth was still full; sticky sweet margarita went everywhere. Robyn lapped after it; the three of them kissed while Brian's hands traced rivulets of margarita over Eve's perfect little tits.

Then Eve's arms circled their shoulders—left arm over Brian, right over Robyn. She formed another death grip—this one just about unbreakable—and pulled both of them firmly against her. She let out a thunderous moan and told them she was coming.

With her fingers buried deep and fingertips, Brian guessed, probably pressed hard against Eve's G-spot, Robyn never let her thumb stop doing the work. The three of them writhed together on the big, cushy love seat, the smell of sweat and of sex intoxicatingly mingling with the margarita magic. Eve cried out over and over again, until she finally begged for mercy under the couple.

Eve's fingers tousled his hair.

"You know," Brian finally said. "We're not bohemians. We do have a bed."

Both Robyn and Eve thought that was a great idea, and for a while they let Brian do all the work. The margaritas were all melted by then, but no one seemed to mind drinking straight from the bottle.

CHAPTER FOURTEEN

TRADING SPOUSES—
SOFT SWAPPING

Let yourself be open and life will be easier.

—BUDDHA

Some couples are happily contained in a neat little one-on-one unit. Others like to play with multiple partners, but as fantasy only. Still others break the rules wide, well, open. Within the genre of open relationships, there are multiple types. Are you interested in an orgy, a free-for-all fucking event? Or an even swap—two partners gently shaken, possibly stirred? For hands-on information, Tristan Taormino penned the guide *Opening Up*. For erotic thoughts on the matter, I like to turn to my bookshelf.

"Counterpane," a short story I penned a while back, features two couples—one hetero and one gay. This story explores voyeurism, exhibitionism, anal and a twist:

"Roll over."

That was something Ry said to her, in just the same way:

"Roll over. Show me that sweet fucking ass of yours."

Now, she watched as the top started to rim his lover. Fucking god. More than talking to Ry about who'd abused this hotel room before, she liked seeing what the two boys would do.

Her heart pounded at the way the brunet roughly pulled apart the blond's cheeks and licked in a tight circle around that tiny pink bud. She clenched her own thighs together. Ry had never done that to her. Nobody had. But she desperately wanted to own that experience, a tongue against her there. Wetness. Warmth. She thought that the sensation alone might make her come. Would it feel like Ry was suckling her clit? Would it make her feel like a boy?

My novel-in-progress *The Trade* focuses solely on a fair swap. I'll take your wife, you take mine:

"He'll fuck you, Jordy," Killian whispered. "In front of everyone. And they'll all know what I know. They'll all know what a dirty little slut you really are."

My cheeks burned, but I wondered if—in spite of his cocky words—he truly could handle the reality of this scene. What would it do to Killian to see another man taking control of me? Breaking through a crowd of people and putting one hand on my shoulder. Forcing me down to my knees. Making me behave.

Christ, it was all Killian's fault. That was the truth. He was the one who had initiated this fantasy. He was the one who made the scene so real in my mind that I could feel a stranger's palm stroking my skin, look up and stare into another man's eyes.

"Oh, they'll all see you," Killian assured me.

I shook my head. I bit my lip. And then I whispered, "Yes."

"Four on the Floor" is a sexy swap in the same room:

The TV stayed on the whole time we were there. Muted, but on. We had crazy sex right on the caramel-colored shag rug in front of it, while heavy metal bands played for us in silence. It was like doing it onstage with Guns & Roses. Surreal, but not a turn-off.

I remember a lot of wetness—her mouth, his mouth, her pussy. I remember Sam leaning against the wood-paneled wall at one point in the evening and watching, just watching the three of us entwined, the TV-glow flickering over us, my slim body stretched out between our new lovers. I felt beloved as their fingers stroked me, as they took turns tasting me, splitting my legs as wide as possible and getting in between. I held my arms over my head and Sam bent down and gripped my wrists tight while Pamela licked at me like a pussycat at a saucer of milk.

Scenes flowed through the night, lubricated by our red-wine daze, and we moved easily from one position to another. Pamela bent on her knees at Sam's feet and brought her mouth to his cock. I worked Andy, bobbing up and down, and after he came for the first time, I moved over to Pamela's side, so we could take turns drinking from Sam. I was reeling with the wonder of it. The illusion that anything was possible. Any position, any desire.

"You like that?" Andy asked when I returned to his side, pointing to Pamela as she sucked off my husband. "You like watching?"

I nodded.

"What else do you like?"

"I like that you spanked her," I confessed in a soft voice.

"Ah," he smiled. "So you're a bad girl, too."

Yet for some inexplicable reason, lately I tend to be drawn to the concept of a good, old-fashioned gang bang, like in "Last Call":

I want the bartender to close and lock the front door at the bar. "What happens in The Local, stays in The Local," I want some wiseass to say. There will be laughter, of the nervous variety, and the men will try not to look into one another's eyes. Because what we're going to do here is a gang bang, and brother, when you say those words aloud, people get jittery.

This isn't non-con, mind you. I am not asking for something from

Last Exit to Brooklyn. *Don't leave me unconscious on an old vinyl car seat behind the bar. Yes, I want the abuse, but I want to revel in every moment. In fact, I want to name the lineup. That's why we have to wait until closing time, when everyone else can leave except for the five men I've chosen.*

The concept of bringing new partners into a relationship doesn't only mean the more the merrier. There are so many emotional aspects to trading. In "Nights Out," Tenille Brown writes:

This was her favorite part, the good-byes, though it probably shouldn't be. The jealous eyes were all but genuine as they issued quick kisses and last-minute rules.

No long embraces…

No funny stories…

Just a fly-by-night fuck is all it is…

…all it will ever be…

It couldn't be normal, she was convinced. She was at least supposed to be more hesitant than she was, but right now her thighs were sliding against each other, and barely able to hold her up.

She was someone else's tonight, and so was he. Only a wall separated their respective escapades. He could hear her moan if he listened closely. She could hear him issue instructions if she tamed her own enjoyment.

In their room, she let her new partner do things she didn't allow her husband to, and that was the most thrilling thing of all, like biting her… as long as he didn't leave any marks. And she let her new partner pull her hair. She didn't even know she liked that part until he grabbed the first handful and now she couldn't get enough.

She imagined her husband was doing the same, breaking the handed down rules. But after all, weren't they both allowed? Wasn't that what this thing was for?

She bent over for a spanking.

She told him, "Just do it, already."

Giselle Renarde's "The Couple with the Dragon Tattoo," features a multicultural MF/FF swap.

Just when I thought Lilliana would kiss my boyfriend's knuckles, she extended his index finger and slowly closed her mouth around it. Ger let out a glorious groan that pulsed inside my core. It was mesmerizing and magnificent to watch her sucking those fingers like five little cocks, devoting care and attention to one and all. She was a minx, that girl. My excitement at having her in our bedroom was surpassed only by the control in Vijee's eyes as she looked on.

Vijee leaned against the bed and patted the mattress. "Come, Marva, sit."

Lilliana nodded in eager acquiescence, her mauve-gray eyes on me all the while. My pussy throbbed. I could have sworn my feet never touched the ground as I cut a quick path to the bed.

We watched in silence as Lilliana unbuttoned Gerry's shirt, sucking his fingers all the while. The sound of his belt unbuckling and his trousers unzipping summoned the sweetest of aches between my legs, and I was certain Vijee recognized my distress. I watched her watching me in the mirrored wardrobe. Vijee and I were so much darker than Lilliana and Gerry, and I wasn't sure what that meant, if it meant anything at all.

"Does this make you jealous?" Vijee asked, as we watched Lilliana pumping Ger's erection in her smallish hand. "My girlfriend jerking off your dear Gerry—are you envious at all?"

"Envious? Yes. I love touching my boyfriend's cock. But jealous? No."

Envy and jealousy can be introduced to a new emotion (perhaps at a cocktail party) often discussed in open relationships. Xan West writes in "Compersion":

It's called compersion. A dyke friend who teaches classes on open relationships taught me the word for it. Compersion. It even sounds dirty. She said that the kind I do is called erotic compersion, when you get off on watching your partner fuck someone else.

Opening up to an open relationship (within whatever confines feels safe to you) often takes time—and a great deal of trust. You can always start small, with words, fantasies and fiction.

TANTALIZING TIPS

• Find a favorite foursome (or "moresome") story to share with your partner. Really put yourself into the plot, pretending that you are one of the players. See how your body reacts to this sensual idea.

• Interested in exploring the option in real life? Check out Tristan Taormino's exquisite *Opening Up: A Guide to Creating and Sustaining Open Relationships.*

• Some partners enjoy swapping in the same room. Others prefer to go solo. Discuss which situation is more of a turn-on for the two of you. (Or try both!)

SYZYGY

ASHLEY LISTER

Syzygy?" Becky repeated. She pronounced the word as Rob had done: *SIZ-uh-jee*. Unable to keep the skepticism from her tone she said, "Are you sure that's the safeword you want us to use tonight?"

He shrugged. "It seems appropriate. Amongst other definitions, it's a Jungian term meaning a union of two opposites."

Becky said nothing. She was wondering how she could fit the word *syzygy* into a casual sentence should she need to call a halt to events later in the evening. She was familiar with using safewords with Rob. When they had been playing S/M games they had employed a variety of safewords such as *Shakespeare* and *carburetor*: words that were extremely unlikely to occur by chance during the passion of an erotic encounter.

But this evening promised to be different on so many levels. This evening they were playing with another couple. And, she supposed, that meant the use of a different type of safeword.

Rob pressed the doorbell.

Becky stiffened. Her heartbeat was already racing. The idea of how the evening might develop tightened her stomach into knots of anticipation. She was grateful when Rob reached out and squeezed her hand with a gesture of understanding and reassurance.

She squeezed back and hoped he didn't notice that her hands were trembling.

"We don't have to do anything that you don't want us to do."

She nodded. He had said the same thing to her many times before. And she had said the same thing to him. It was a credo by which they both lived. And it wasn't that she didn't want to do this with him. She was only hesitant because she had no idea what the evening might entail.

The door opened.

Dan and Jan stood before them. They were smiling warm welcomes that looked as exciting as the pictures Becky had seen on the swinging website where they first organized this meet. The four of them shook hands, bussed cheeks with smiles and greeted one another with hurried welcomes that told Becky the couple were as nervous as she and Rob.

The artificiality of being kissed on the cheek by a stranger struck Becky as unpleasant and unwanted and she wondered why she had ever desired something like this evening's planned encounter. She kept the thought to herself, remembering that there would always be an opportunity to use the safeword if she chose. At the moment she figured it was more likely that nervousness was dictating her likes and dislikes more than any genuine enjoyment.

"Drinks?"

"Yes, please."

Dan played a generous host, escorting them into a stylish lounge with muted lighting, a single settee and a plasma TV. Jan kept glancing at Becky and Rob, her gaze flashing between one and the other with hungry enthusiasm.

And, while she hadn't really enjoyed the artificiality of the kiss on the cheek, Becky did like being the object of the woman's sexual interest.

She took a seat in the center of the single settee and accepted a vodka from Dan.

Jan sat next to Becky and gave her a reassuring smile. "Nervous?"

"A little," Becky admitted. "This is our first time."

Jan placed a hand on Becky's knee.

The sensation of the woman's warm fingertips touching the bare skin of her flesh made the inner muscles of Becky's sex clench hungrily. Of all the things that she had expected to happen this evening, the surge of arousal from another woman's interest and touch was not one of them.

She wasn't sure if she was comfortable with those responses.

She struggled to try to remember the safeword that Rob had suggested. Her mind was momentarily blank and all she could recollect was that it was some pretentious word that she would never use during the course of normal conversation.

Silently she cursed him for being such a word snob.

"I'm sure we'll have fun," Jan insisted. "We won't do anything you don't want to do."

Dan joined his partner on the settee and nodded for Rob to join Becky. The four of them sat in front of the large TV screen, each holding their drinks as they chatted about the journey and then went on to discuss the pros and cons of the various websites they all knew.

The air was rich with the scents of perfume, the sounds of strained laughter and the tension of simmering sexual excitement. Becky silently savored the pleasure of being in the company of broadminded adults who shared her desire to explore new and unconventional ways of achieving satisfaction. The prospect of what might happen as the evening developed made gooseflesh prickle her arms.

Syzygy, Becky remembered suddenly. *A Jungian term meaning a union of two opposites. How the hell am I supposed to say that without it sounding like a safeword?* She could imagine herself screaming the word in terror as she bolted from Dan and Jan's home. The idea was so comical she almost blurted laughter.

"You two were interested in a soft swap, weren't you?"

Becky nodded as she sipped her vodka.

She had scoured through several online glossaries to understand all the terminology in the sexually adventurous world of swapping and sharing but it was like learning a different language. There were so many new phrases and euphemisms it seemed impossible to keep abreast of them all. No one had *sex* on these sites—couples simply *played.* According to her favorite site a *soft swap* was a situation where two couples played in the same room, but they only played with their original partners. Excitement came from the exhibitionist pleasure of performing for a small audience, and the voyeuristic excitement of seeing another couple playing in such close proximity.

"Soft swap," Becky repeated. "That's right."

The words tasted dangerous.

Considering the glint she could see in Jan's eyes, she knew that the other woman understood exactly what she was hoping to get from the evening. The idea that they were both in tune with the other's needs was sufficiently exciting to make her stomach knot with fresh arousal.

"I think a soft swap is the right way for any couple to test the waters of the lifestyle," Jan confided. She glanced back to Dan. Her smile showed a solidarity of spirit. "It's how we started. It's a favorite that we keep going back to when we want to get to know another couple."

Her fingers returned to Becky's leg. This time she squeezed higher up the thigh. Becky was aware of her sex growing moist and warm. Her breasts suddenly ached with longing and she realized her nipples were painfully hard and pushing against the tight fabric of her blouse.

"Rest assured," Jan promised, "if we think you guys are going too fast for us, we'll say something. I trust you'll do the same for us?"

Becky nodded.

Dan had a remote in his hand. He pointed it toward the TV set and said, "Are we okay to have a little something playing in the background?"

As no one objected, he pressed the PLAY button and the TV came to life.

Becky was not surprised that the film was a porno. She would have been disturbed if the couple had decided to develop the mood by playing a musical or an action thriller. Under the circumstances a porno seemed like the most appropriate choice of film genre.

But it did come as a surprise to her that the film starred Jan.

The opening screen showed Jan's face in the throes of ecstasy. The wobbling camera angle moved back to show that her shoulders were bare. Then it showed her boobs. They were round and inviting and looked as though they had been sculpted beneath the knife of a perfectionist surgeon.

Becky squirmed with a small spike of jealousy.

As the camera panned back, it revealed that Jan was completely naked. Her stomach was flat. Her muscles were small but beautifully defined. Her pussy was completely free from hair. Between her legs she held a buzzing dildo and pressed it deep into the center of her sex.

Becky stifled a gasp.

She had seen pornos before. But she had never looked at erotic images of someone else while sitting next to her on a settee. The idea was enough to make her sex feel oily with anticipation.

Rob crossed his legs.

Jan laughed. It wasn't an unkind sound. She reached across Becky and placed a hand on Rob's thigh. Becky could smell the lightly floral fragrance of the woman's perfume. She drank the scent greedily. It was like inhaling raw sex appeal.

"There's no need to hide the fact that you've been turned on," Jan assured Rob. "In truth, I'm flattered. Dan is probably excited by the fact that you're excited. And I suspect that Becky isn't repulsed by your arousal."

Slowly, with an apologetic grin, Rob lowered the protective leg.

Becky wondered how she should respond to the situation. A woman she had known for only a few minutes was encouraging Rob to be aroused at a film of her wanking. She reflected on the situation for a moment and then realized this was just as thrilling as she had hoped it would be when she and Rob arranged to meet the other couple. She reached to touch Rob's leg, eager to reassure him that she was sharing his excitement. Her hand touched high and, once she had given his thigh a reassuring squeeze, she allowed her fingers to slip a little higher and brush the thrust of his excitement.

As she had guessed, he was already hard.

His erection twitched beneath her touch.

Rob sighed.

Becky cast a nervous glance toward Jan and Dan. She was worried that the noise might be too loud. She was worried that stroking her boyfriend's bulge might have overstepped the boundaries of polite activity in the home of their new friends. Even though she knew she and Rob were only visiting Dan and Jan with the intention of participating in a soft swap, it still seemed prudent to make sure she hadn't gone too far in exploiting their hospitality.

Jan was bent over Dan's lap.

Becky couldn't see what was happening but she recognized the movement of Jan's head sliding back and forth.

On the plasma screen Jan was grunting through a noisy orgasm. The dildo was buried deep into her sex, and she was writhing happily on its thickness. On the video, Becky could hear Dan murmuring words of encouragement from behind the camera.

And on the settee beside her, she saw Dan had now turned to grin at her while Jan sucked his cock.

The sudden rush of arousal was fluid and delicious.

Becky grinned for him. At the same time she reached back to Rob and her fingers again found his erection. He was still hard and she tugged his zip downward.

Rob's hand caught her wrist. He leaned close and pressed a kiss against her neck beneath her ear.

"Are you sure about this?" he whispered.

Instead of answering with words, Becky released his erection from his pants. His length was already at full hardness and so she simply stroked her fingers up and down him with loving affection.

"Nice cock," Jan muttered.

Becky hadn't even noticed that the woman was now facing them. Jan spoke while her lips were kissing the tip of Dan's substantial length. The woman's tongue lapped at the glossy flesh of Dan's hardness.

"If you need lube or anything, we've got tubes in those drawers," Jan said. She nodded toward a corner unit. "Or if you need your drinks refilled or—"

Becky shook her head as she stood up. She continued holding onto Rob's erection as she said, "I think I've got everything I need right here."

Jan giggled. "I think you have," she agreed.

Becky's skirt was short and she wore no panties beneath. Raising the hem slightly, exposing her bare buttocks to the room, she eased herself slowly over Rob's lap.

Her loins turned to fire when she heard Jan draw an excited breath.

Dan murmured, "Go for it, girl."

Becky held her breath.

The air was so thick with excitement she was having difficulty drawing it into her lungs. She hesitated over Rob's erection, savoring the pleasure of having his rounded end pushing at her wetness. The moment was so filled with electric pleasure she could feel her knees beginning to quiver from the experience.

It had crossed her mind that she could follow Jan's example. Jan had been sucking on Dan. Becky could have simply sucked on Rob's erection. But, while that idea held some appeal, Becky did not want to appear as though she was simply mimicking the woman's actions.

She held the base of Rob's erection and rested the sopping split of her sex over his end. Her heartbeat raced when she glanced at Jan and Dan and saw they were both watching.

"Is there anything either of us can do to help?" Jan asked.

Becky laughed. "Don't tempt me with offers like that." And, with those words, she pushed herself heavily onto Rob's length.

The sensation was sublime. His erection filled her. She felt an immediate rush of satisfaction begin to envelop her—more profound than anything she could usually expect from simply sitting on his cock. Gut instinct told her that she would only need to slide slowly up and down his erection a couple more times and the orgasm would scorch through her body.

While that prospect was appealing, and she could have happily ridden up and down on Rob's length for the remainder of the evening, it crossed Becky's mind that she wasn't providing her audience with much to enjoy.

Casually, she slipped open the button on her skirt and allowed the zipper to pull open. The skirt fell from her hips leaving her lower half completely bare. Grinning for Jan and Dan as she slid up and down Rob's erection, Becky teased open the buttons on her blouse.

The other couple made sounds of excited encouragement as Becky shrugged off the blouse and revealed herself topless.

"You do realize," Jan told Dan, "that now she's naked, that means we have to take our clothes off."

Thrilled by the way the evening was developing, Becky squeezed her inner muscles tight around Rob's erection. With a wave of encroaching bliss, she relished the rush of the climax that seared through her loins.

Three hours later they stood on the doorstep preparing to leave.

This time, when Jan and Becky kissed farewell, Becky could sense that there was friendship rather than the artificiality of their former faux greeting. The pressure of the woman's lips on hers made Becky wonder what else she and Jan could do in the pursuit of pleasure.

"We'll have to do this again," Jan said earnestly.

Becky nodded. "We must. Maybe more."

"More?" Jan teased. "How much more would you want to do?"

"It depends what the syzygy is like."

Jan looked momentarily puzzled.

Beside her Rob was frowning and Becky knew he would have a perplexing journey home trying to figure out whether she'd said the safeword because she didn't want to repeat the experience of the soft swap, or simply because she'd found an opportunity to use the word.

And, she supposed, by the time he asked her, *she* might have worked out how she felt about the experience and whether or not she wanted it to happen again.

CHAPTER FIFTEEN

MIND YOUR MA'AMS—
FEMME DOMME

Disguise our bondage as we will,
'Tis woman, woman, rules us still.

—THOMAS MOORE

For a moment, I thought I didn't have any femme domme clips of my own to share. I told myself, *You don't really write femme domme, now do you, silly girl?* And then I thought, *Oh, excuse me. What did you just say, little voice?* Because my New Stories folder— yes, that's the ever-so-clever title on the lip—is filled to the rim with f/d stories!

Why?

Well, I have this funny internal glitch. Occasionally, I will meet a man and think, *Dom. You are a total Dom, Sir.* And other times, I will meet a man and think, *What you really need is to have some woman, some ice-cold woman, take charge of you.* In either case, I go write a story. Like "Plucked," which features a man named Sandy who meets his match:

He chuckles, nervously. When was Sandy last nervous in front of a girl? Sometime circa the '90s, I'd have to guess. "I'm here," he says, "for good."

"That's my only option? For good?"

I feel as if Sandy and I are in some way connected. Our hearts beat faster at her dark, slow words. My mental pleas of Run, Sandy, run, *have changed in a quarter note to* Be bad for her, Sandy. Go home with her and be bad.

He looks at me, and I see that although his face is composed, his eyes are begging. I pour him a shot and refill her glass, buying him time. I've never been nice to Sandy before, but the look he gives me is pure gratitude, worth more than any crumpled-up buck tip he might leave on the bar.

In "Broken," my main character finds something he didn't even know was missing:

She had cuffs in her hand, as if magically, and she dangled them in front of his face. "You want me to tie you to the bed?" he asked. He'd never played like that before.

"No," she said. "I want to tie you down."

His cock responded as if she'd spoken directly to it instead of to him. What was going on? He'd never even thought to do things kinky before. Most of the girls he dated were so young that simply the act of fucking was exciting to them.

"Are you game?" She put one hand on his dick. He was rock hard. "You seem game."

"I was going out," he said, to give himself a second to think.

She nodded. "I know. You were going out. Take off your shirt."

He could stop this charade at any second. He could tell her she was over the top, rebounding, using him to get her aggressions out. But he took off his shirt anyway.

Some people might start out with their fantasies online, like the character in "Flash," from *Bondage on a Budget*:

In the online room, she was a dominant. She held court and the people around her scurried to obey. I did, as well. I'm not proud. But I was able to capture her interest with my remarks, and ultimately she invited me to join her in a private room. Once alone, we continued our fantasy play. She had a camera. She tied me up and took pictures, spread my legs and observed my cunt under a magnifying glass. I liked it, enjoyed being exposed. It was safe for me since all of it was a farce.

At the end, after we both took turns climaxing (I'm getting pretty good at typing one-handed), she asked me to meet her.

Dominatrixes are everywhere. Emilie Paris writes in "Underwater":

Some of my friends would be shocked by my tastes. I simply don't look the part of the dominatrix. I'm slight, but I'm tough. My lovers have always submitted to my needs. There's never been a question about it. I call to them, the ones that like to bow down. I don't seek them out, they come to me.

N. T. Morley spills a craving for a dom in "Date Night":

She flipped through the channels and quickly settled on a tall ice-blonde Dominatrix in a tight latex dress smoking a cigarette in a long holder while a very cute and very nude brunette worshipped the Mistress's shiny knee-high boots.

Yum. That would do rather nicely, thanks.

The domme in "Working Late," by Andrea Dale, has multiple instructions for her man:

His chest heaved when he saw what I'd packed for him. What I had planned for him.

"Tell me what you've found."

He tried to speak, failed, cleared his throat and started again. "A pair of small clamps—nipple clamps. A butt plug, and a packet of lube. Ma'am."

"Tell me what you're going to do with them."

Sometimes I gave orders, but often Jack was smart enough to know what I wanted. I mean, duh, they weren't unusual toys. Besides, having him describe what was going to happen heightened the anticipation—for both of us.

My breasts felt heavy, swollen beneath my silk blouse. I didn't need to look to know my own nipples were clear against the soft fabric.

"I'm going to go to the men's room and put the clamps on my nipples. I'll probably have to massage my nipples a little to get them ready for the clamps." Jack looked down at the items on his desk. *"I'll coat the plug with lube, and also my fingers, and open myself up before inserting the plug."*

"Will you like that?"

It wasn't an easy question and didn't have an easy answer. He had a love-hate relationship with the plug, craved the sensation while aware of how it looked, what it meant.

"Yes, Ma'am," he said.

"Then what?"

"I'll come back to my desk, and when you see me, you'll call me with further instructions."

"Good boy. Go on, then."

Jax Baynard's "Meltdown" also takes the domme's point of view:

I snapped the whip a couple of times, limbering up, trying to think calmly. What was he after? If I knew what it was I could either give it to him or not, my choice. But I didn't know, and the anger and the hurt running beneath it, the hurt I was trying frantically to stay on top of, made it impossible to think rationally. So I hit him. Despite my threats, I pulled a few punches. I pulled all of them, actually, practicing restraint as a cautionary measure. After a minute or two he said conversationally, "You probably deserved it."

"What did you just say?" I asked.

"You heard me," he said, which, of course, I had.

I snapped the whip, the fine tip at the end making a crack. If I hit him like that, he would bleed instantly. It was the same as being sliced open with a knife. They don't pay me so much for nothing. I was good enough to be blunt, hitting him hard without breaking the skin. He jerked with the force of it.

"You're probably a real cunt," he said pleasantly. "I've thought so for years."

Those might not be *my* first words to a domme with a whip. But there are so many different ways people work to get what they want. If you're a woman who has always craved control—or a closet sub who craves giving up the reins—take a deep breath, approach your lover and confess.

You might wind up getting more than you want. You might get what you deserve.

TANTALIZING TIPS

- Pay attention to the media. There are so many examples of domme women to learn from. Check out the ads for Justin Timberlake's naughty 901 Tequila ads—foreplay in seconds.

- Clothes don't simply make the man, they make the man beg. The right outfit can transform a woman into a fierce domme as quickly as you can slip on those thigh-high vinyl boots.

- Don't leave home (or enter the bedroom) without a safeword.

NO SHAME

DANTE DAVIDSON

T here's no shame in asking for what you want."

She said the words as she walked around me. I stood naked in front of her. My wrists were cuffed and attached to a beam over my head. I could feel her breath when she came close, when she ran the tip of her fingernail down my spine.

"There's no shame in giving in. No shame in begging."

My eyes were closed, but that didn't matter. She had put a blindfold on me as soon as I'd entered the room. I hoped like hell she could not tell from my expression that I didn't agree with her. I ought to have known better.

"You think I'm wrong, don't you?"

No, Mistress. Yes, Mistress. What was the right answer? What answer would win me what I desired?

"Don't you?"

It wasn't her fingernail tracing down my back now. That mean device was the tip of a crop. I knew that from experience. I sucked in my breath and waited for the first stroke. None came.

"Say the words with me," she instructed in a singsong tone that made me immediately fearful. She was being playful. That did not bode well for me. "There's no shame."

"There's no shame," I parroted back to her, lying. No shame? Who was she kidding? Didn't she know by now that the whole game, the whole fucking situation, was based on shame? This scene wouldn't be the same without that filament of emotion, burning a bright incandescent blue within me.

"No shame in begging," she continued.

"No shame in begging," I whispered.

"So beg me."

I bit my lip.

"Beg me."

I turned my head away from her voice. I couldn't. I wouldn't. She could tie me up. She could whip me. She could make tears streak my face. But I would not ask her to do those things to me. I would not...

The crop struck once, and I felt as if I had won. Until she said again: "Beg me."

My cock was a throbbing beast between my legs. The sound of her voice alone was enough to make me hard. Adding the pain of the punishment could make me come. But she didn't keep going. She was pushing hard on my boundaries today. Truculently, I pushed back with my willful disobedience.

"You're not paying attention," she said, and she sounded sad. I could picture exactly what she looked like. I'd seen her fully for a second when I entered the room—glossy black latex catsuit. High-heeled boots. Dark hair up in a neat twist. Smoldering charcoal eye shadow. Plenty of mascara. Then she'd told me to strip and put a blindfold on me.

"You know what happens when you don't pay attention."

I flinched. I could guess. I heard the clink of ice in her glass, smelled the whiskey when she brought the tumbler close to my nose. Then I felt cold fingers behind me, and I knew what she was doing. The ice cube against my asshole made me grind my teeth. My cock got harder, if that was possible. I set my feet wider apart. She probed me with the ice, and I felt drops of precome leak from my cock.

"I hurt you and then I fuck you when you don't pay attention," she said.

I understood what she meant. She was going to whip me with her crop and then fuck me with her strap-on. My arms ached from the bindings, but I didn't care.

"But only if you tell me what you want," she told me. "Only if you beg."

One of her hands caressed my cock now, cold fingers working up and down. Her other hand continued to run the ice cube around my asshole until the heat of my body melted the cube completely. I wanted what she'd promised. I needed what she said.

"Please," I said, knowing that wasn't enough. She wouldn't be satisfied. She's never satisfied.

"Please what?"

"Please do what you said." I hated myself for being unable to speak the words.

She sighed. I heard her heels on the floor. She was leaving the room, leaving me, and suddenly I started to feel frantic. I began to babble. "Please, Ma'am. Please, Mistress. Do those things to me. Hurt me. Fuck me. Take me. There's no shame," I continued, words tumbling. "No shame."

She returned. She got so close to me. I felt the crop again, felt her running the tip between my asscheeks, felt her probing me.

"You're so sweet when you lie," she said, and then she began.

CHAPTER SIXTEEN

24/7—

LIVING A KINKY LIFE

Dost thou love life? Then do not squander time, for that is the stuff life is made of.

—BENJAMIN FRANKLIN

Y ou don't have to be a writer of erotica to live a kinky life. You only have to possess an imagination. That's the sound bite, the one fortune-cookie wisp of wisdom I hope to leave with you. When you start to explore what you want—what you need—you can turn your whole world upside down. And that's a good thing. Thinking about feeling sexy all of the time is surreal. Imagine dressing for yourself and for your lover, finding the toys and the tools that arouse the two (or more) of you.

Soon you'll realize that truth might not necessarily be stranger than fiction...but it definitely can be just as fucking sexy. In fact, I think real sex—real-life sex with all the unexpected qualities that go with it—is far more erotic than a make-believe world.

Take risks. There are two words to tattoo onto your forearm. If you've never watched porn, rent an X-rated movie together. If you've never tried a toy, visit a sex shop (in life or online). Read each other smut out loud. Leave sexy notes (where you know the intended reader will find them). Give into your desires. Talk dirty. All the time. Make double entendres. Then triple them.

Feel your heart race. Feel your body respond.

In the BDSM world, there is a concept of living a 24/7 life—24/7 as the master or slave in a relationship. But we're all living 24/7 here. Nobody's checking out at 23. Nobody's cutting their weeks short to 6. Make your relationship what you crave. Let your cup runneth over.

Live a kinky life.

TANTALIZING TIPS

- Read erotica, eat exotic foods, watch foreign fuck films, dress in the clothes of your dreams, push against your boundaries, fall into your fantasies. Turn your volume to eleven.

- Borrow my glasses for a minute so that you can see sex everywhere you go. Really, it's all a mindset. Once you decide to embrace a kinky lifestyle, the opportunities won't bother knocking at your door. They'll knock you down and have their way with you on the living room floor. Let them.

IS THAT MAN BOTHERING YOU?

ALISON TYLER

Is that man bothering you?"

I'm standing in front of my closet, trying to decide what to wear. I don't even turn to face Sam, but I can feel him right behind me, waiting for my response.

"Which man?" I ask, as I reach for my favorite red dress.

He puts his hands out to stop me, and in seconds, my wrists are pinned behind my back. I was silly to think I could get away with walking around in only my black satin bra and panties when Sam was nearby.

"The man touching you," he says as his fingertips dip into my knickers, as his pointer parts my nether lips to feel the wetness between. "Is he bothering you? Should I do something about him?"

Touching me. Yes, a man is touching me. Sam has his free hand running up and down my split, and I nearly buckle. I would, except he has me standing at attention with his hand on my wrists. I bow, wishing we were close to the bed, wishing I could collapse and luxu-riate in the way he manhandles me. But he's having none of my wishes. This is about Sam, mind-fucking me as he finger-fucks my pussy. I keep myself from begging. We're not even close.

He pulls me in front of the mirror over my dresser and makes me watch him. His fingers are sticky with my juices, and he runs his fingertips over my lips then kisses me. I taste myself in his kiss. He releases my wrists, but I keep them in place, staring as he pulls my bra down in front, revealing my breasts. He pinches my nipples—first the right, then the left—and I close my eyes and sigh.

Sam doesn't miss a trick. "Open your eyes."

I obey, immediately.

"I'm waiting for an answer."

"I forgot the question."

He nudges me with his erection. I would drop to my knees and suck him, except he hasn't asked me to.

"Is that man bothering you?"

"Which one?" I ask, and his eyes glow. I've taken back a tiny bit of the power. "The one who just had his fingers in my snatch? Or the one who's jacking off in the chair, thinking about fucking my asshole."

Sam stares at me, and I wonder how he will respond. I don't have to wonder for long.

"The one who's about to spank you," he says, and I feel my pussy get even wetter than before. He leads me to the bed, bends me over the mattress, drags my panties down my thighs. Seconds ago, I was hoping he'd bend me over the bed. Now I'm not so sure. I feel his hand trace over the curves of my ass, and I relax, thinking he's only going to spank me with his palm. When will I ever learn? Sam never does what I expect. He pulls a paddle from under the mattress, and in seconds I am writhing from the blows. His strokes heat my skin and make my pussy pulse. I'm useless at behaving. I always wish I could.

I never can.

He hisses for me to stay still, and I want to say, "I'm trying." But I'm smart enough to keep my mouth shut. Still, I squirm as he spanks me, and soon I have tested his limits. He grips me up, pushes me farther on the bed, buckles my wrists into cuffs and binds me easily in place.

What's next? I don't ask. I wait. But Sam says, "That man's ready."

"Which one?" I'm panting.

"The one who's going to take that sweet ass of yours."

Sam surprises me, slipping a blindfold over my eyes. I tense. Losing my sight makes me nervous and Sam knows that.

He has me on my stomach, knees under my body. He's using lube, a lot of lube, and I feel myself open up for him. What was I doing five minutes ago? Attempting to get dressed for a party? Now my ass is hot and throbbing and I'm about to get speared.

"Open your mouth," Sam says. "The other man wants you to suck him off while you're getting that tight asshole reamed."

Oh, god. I can feel myself getting closer to climaxing. Sam's words are pure magic. He takes me higher and higher. I open my mouth, thinking we're playing pretend. I'm going to suck off an imaginary cock, and then I feel the tip in my mouth. How is that possible? Sam's behind me, lubing my back door. I run my tongue around the head and realize—synthetic. Sam's got me sucking a dildo. But his story-telling skills keep me believing, even when I know the cock's plastic. He tells me that there are two men in the room. One about to take my asshole, the other fucking my face.

I groan around the toy cock, and Sam uses that moment to push the head of his own rod inside of me.

"Is that man bothering you?" he whispers, as he fucks two of my holes in tandem. I slur words around the dildo, not even knowing what

I'm saying, and Sam says, "I'll make him stop if you want me to."

I shake my head. I want it all. I never want it to stop.

Sam pauses in his action, surprising me once more. He slips one of my vibrators into my pussy then flicks on the motor. When he resumes fucking my ass, I am transported. Three holes filled, and Sam's still talking.

"You look good like this, pretty girl," he says. "You look good with your holes being used. You look perfect bound and blindfolded. We should have parties like this more often." I moan around the cock in my mouth, grind my hips on the dildo in my pussy and contract on Sam's cock. I'm being gangbanged by the man I love, and I have a record-breaking orgasm when the pleasure finally crashes over me.

Sam lets go of the toy, and I let the cock fall from my mouth. He grips both of my hips in his big hands, driving into my ass as fast and as hard as if he were fucking my cunt. I tip my head back and forth, and the blindfold comes off. I see our reflection in the mirror over the dresser, and I think we look like porn stars. Shimmering in heat.

He pulls out and comes all over my ass, then uses his palm to rub the glossy liquid into my skin. When he reaches for the cuffs, I pull away. He was going to free me, but I don't want to be freed.

"Sam," I say, "that man...that man's bothering me."

"Which one?"

"The one who's going to take a shower and then get back in bed with me to sixty-nine."

"Why's he bothering you?" Sam asks.

"He's not moving fast enough," I tell him, and Sam slaps my ass and laughs.

ABOUT THE AUTHORS

CLARICE ALEXANDER spends a lot of time in dressing rooms. She is currently working on a novel about sex and shopping, her two most favorite naughty passions.

JANINE ASHBLESS (janineashbless.blogspot.com) is a multipublished author of (mostly supernatural) erotica. Her stories have been published by—among others—Spice, Black Lace, Nexus, Xcite, Ellora's Cave, Samhain, Mischief, Sweetmeats and Cleis (including the anthologies *Frenzy, Carnal Machines* and *Thrones of Desire*). She lives in England.

VIDA BAILEY (heatsuffused.blogspot.com) is a lady writer from Ireland who writes stories when the whim takes her. She has published work in *Love at First Sting, Dirtyville, Steamlust* and *Bound by Lust*.

By day, **JAX BAYNARD** is a financial investment advisor. By night, she makes her own (and her clients') fantasies come true. This part-time dominatrix's short fiction has appeared in *With This Ring, I Thee Bed, Pleasure Bound*, online and in several literary journals.

One half of a happily married couple who have rediscovered each other, **LIZA BENNET** began chronicling her reawakened sex life after a ten-year drought on her blog Always Each Other. Her work has appeared on the websites The Good Men Project and Fleshbot. She enjoys writing both fiction and nonfiction erotica.

HELENA BLACK lives in Texas. She loves reading dirty stories, taking pictures of beautiful people, and good coffee. You can find her work in such wonderful anthologies as *Got a Minute?: 60 Second Erotica* and *Frenzy: 60 Stories of Sudden Sex*.

CHEYENNE BLUE's (cheyenneblue.com) erotica has appeared in over sixty anthologies including *Best Women's Erotica, Mammoth Best New Erotica, Cowboy Lust: Erotic Romance for Women* and *Lesbian Lust*. The darkness before dawn is her favorite time of day.

She's done it again! At thirty-seven, **ANGELL BROOKS** has somehow managed to fluke her way into another collection with some amazing erotica writers, and she couldn't be happier. The road trip to the top of the charts continues from Toronto, with dreams of tropical climates, cabana boys and tequila.

TENILLE BROWN's (therealtenille.com) smut is featured in nearly fifty print anthologies including *Chocolate Flava 1* and *3, Curvy Girls, Going Down, Best Bondage Erotica 2011* and *2012, Sapphic Planet, Suite Encounters, Open* and *Best Lesbian Erotica 2013*. The Southern wife and mother writes for Mischief Books.

Although **ANDREA DALE** (AndreaDaleAuthor.com) sometimes dabbles in flash fiction, she doesn't necessarily believe that brevity is the soul of wit. Has she tantalized you? Do you want to know more? Visit her online and see what else she has to say.

DANTE DAVIDSON's short stories have appeared in anthologies including *Bondage, Naughty Stories from A to Z, Best Bondage Erotica, The Merry XXXmas Book of Erotica, Luscious* and *Sweet Life*. With Alison Tyler, he is the coauthor of *Bondage on a Budget* and *Secrets for Great Sex After 50*.

LUCIA DIXON's work has appeared in *Girls on the Go*, *Gone Is the Shame* and *Naughty Stories from A to Z.*

JUSTINE ELYOT (justineelyot.com) arrived on the erotica scene for the last gasp of Black Lace with her UK bestseller, *On Demand*. Since then, she has been published by a variety of imprints, including Carina Press, Xcite Books, Cleis Press and Total E-Bound, among others.

As a naughty girl on a journey of self-discovery as an erotic writer, **TAMSIN FLOWERS** is as keen to entertain her readers as she is to explore every aspect of female erotica. She writes lighthearted stories that are perfect for reading on your own or with someone in whom you have more than a passing interest…

SHANNA GERMAIN (shannagermain.com) claims the titles of writer, editor, leximaven, vorpal blonde and Schrodinger's brat. Her most recent publications include *Bound by Lust* and *The Lure of Dangerous Women*. She is currently the coeditor of *Geek Love: An Anthology of Full Frontal Nerdity.*

ELISE HEPNER (elisehepner.com) writes smutty goodness for Ellora's Cave, Xcite and Excessica. She's appeared in several Cleis anthologies including *Gotta Have It* and *Best Bondage Erotica 2012*. She lives with her husband and two clingy kitties in Maryland.

GEORGIA E. JONES graduated with an MFA from Mills College. Her stories have appeared in the *Santa Barbara Review* and the literary magazine *Estero,* as well as in *Alison's Wonderland* and *Morning, Noon and Night*. Her first novella, *The Earl Takes a Lover,* was published by Harlequin Spice. She lives in Northern California.

DILO KEITH is a polymorphously perverse pansexual queer who recently discovered writing as way to express a lifelong fascination with sexuality and a multi-decade interest in BDSM. It felt great the first time, so Dilo did it again, first alone, later with friends and eventually in public.

CJ LEMIRE lives near the juncture of the New England woods and the deep blue sea. By day he toils away in the wacky world of high tech. In his spare time, he listens to the voices in his head and writes down their kinky stories.

ASHLEY LISTER is a prolific writer of erotic fiction having written more than two dozen full-length erotic novels and over a hundred short stories. Aside from regularly blogging about writing erotica, Ashley also teaches creative writing in the Northwest of England.

KRISTINA LLOYD (kristinalloyd.co.uk) writes novels for the erotica imprint Black Lace. Her short stories have appeared in numerous anthologies, including several "best of" collections, and her work has been translated into German, Dutch and Japanese. She has a master's degree in Twentieth Century Literature and lives in Brighton, United Kingdom.

JENNY LYN (authorjennylyn.com) is a writer of naughty stories and a lover of all things Southern, including her tiny hometown in north-central Florida. She has an ebook out now, *Saving Sydney*; short stories in the upcoming erotic anthologies *Best Women's Erotica 2013* and *Felt Tips*, and many more things in the works.

K. LYNN (writerklynn.com) has been a longtime fan of the erotica market, sneaking in reading time when no one was watching. She enjoys subverting the gender stereotypes in her writing and looks forward to exploring that more in the future. When she's not writing short stories, she's working on her novels.

SAMANTHA MALLERY's writing has appeared in the magazines *Zed* and *Eye* and in the anthology *Batteries Not Included*.

SOMMER MARSDEN's (sommermarsden.blogspot.com) short work has appeared in over one hundred print anthologies. And she's not done yet. Sommer is the author of *Restless Spirit, Big Bad* and numerous other erotic novels.

JULIA MOORE is the coauthor of the bestselling book *The Other Rules*, a spoof of the dating guide *The Rules*. Her erotic short stories have appeared in *Sweet Life, Tasting Her* and on the website goodvibes.com.

MOLLY MOORE (mollysdailykiss.com) is the writer of one of the United Kingdom's most successful sex blogs. She has had her work exhibited at the Festival Of Erotic Arts (2012) in Edinburgh and was a 2012 Erotic Awards finalist. Most of her writing is based on her own experiences and contains strong autobiographical content.

N. T. MORLEY (ntmorley.com) is the author of twenty-four published novels of erotic dominance and submission, as well as short fiction that has appeared in many other anthologies—much of it collected in Morley's three published collections from Renaissance Ebooks.

EMILIE PARIS's first novel, *Valentine* was made into an audiotape by Passion Press. She abridged the seventeenth-century novel, *The Carnal Prayer Mat* for Passion Press, which won a *Publisher's Weekly* best audio award in the "Sexcapades" category.

GISELLE RENARDE (donutsdesires.blogspot.com) is a queer Canadian, avid volunteer, contributor to more than one hundred short-story anthologies and author of numerous books, including *Anonymous, Nanny State* and *My Mistress' Thighs.*

TERESA NOELLE ROBERTS writes romantic erotica and erotic romance for lusty romantics of all persuasions. Her work has appeared in *The Big Book of Bondage*; *Best Bondage Erotica 2011, 2012* and *2013; Orgasmic; Playing with Fire* and other anthologies with provocative titles. She writes erotic romance for Samhain and Phaze.

THOMAS S. ROCHE's (thomasroche.com) novel *The Panama Laugh* was a finalist for the Horror Writers' Association's Bram Stoker Award. Roche's other books include the *Noirotica* series of erotic crime anthologies and four collections of fantasy and horror.

ELISA SHARONE's heretofore super-secret sex writing has soaked hundreds of thousands of panties across the globe. She's wandering a new path, dipping into the deepest, darkest recesses of her imagination to bring readers brain-melting erotica that leaves them gasping for more.

J. SINCLAIRE is a Toronto-based writer by profession but erotic by nature. Her work has appeared in anthologies such as *Cheeky Spanking Stories, Lips Like Sugar* and *The Happy Birthday Book of Erotica.*

CHARLOTTE STEIN (charlottestein.net) has written over thirty short stories, novellas and novels, including an entry in *Best New Erotica 10.* Her collection of short stories was named one of the best erotic romances of 2009 by Michelle Buonfiglio, and she's also published a novel, *Control.*

DONNA GEORGE STOREY (DonnaGeorgeStorey.com) is the author of an erotic novel, *Amorous Woman,* based on her own experiences living in Japan. Her adults-only tales have appeared in numerous places including *Best Women's Erotica, Penthouse, Alison's Wonderland* and *Morning, Noon and Night.*

SOPHIA VALENTI (sophiavalenti.blogspot.com) is the author of *Indecent Desires,* an erotic novella of spanking and submission, and her fiction has appeared in the anthologies *Alison's Wonderland* and *With This Ring, I Thee Bed,* as well as *Kiss My Ass, Skirting the Issue, Bad Ass* and *Torn.*

SHARON WACHSLER (sharonwachsler.com) is always delighted when her erotica appears in an Alison Tyler anthology, including, most recently, *Sudden Sex* and *The Big Book of Bondage.*

KAT WATSON (blog.katwatson.com) is a mom, wife, crafter and chef. She enjoys all couplings and settings. Love is almost always the reason, but the surrounding details fascinate her. Figuring out the talking voices in her head is one of her greatest pleasures. Finding a fabulous bottle of red wine is, too.

XAN WEST is the pseudonym of an NYC BDSM/sex educator and writer. Xan's "First Time Since" won honorable mention for the 2008 NLA John Preston Short Fiction Award. Xan's work appears all over, including *Best Lesbian Erotica 2011* & *2012, Hot Daddies, Pleasure Bound, Hurts So Good* and *Say Please.*

ERIC WILLIAMS has written for assorted erotic anthologies including *Sweet Life, Three-Way, Luscious,* and *Naughty Stories from A to Z.*

CORA ZANE (corazane.com) lives in an area of northern Louisiana known as "out in the sticks." Her work has been published by Ellora's Cave, Cobblestone Press, Wild Child Publishing and various other independent and electronic publishers.

ABOUT THE EDITOR

Called "a trollop with a laptop" by *East Bay Express,* "a literary siren" by Good Vibrations and "the mistress of literary erotica" by Violet Blue, **ALISON TYLER** is naughty and she knows it.

Over the past two decades, Ms. Tyler has written more than twenty-five explicit novels, including *Tiffany Twisted, Melt with You* and *The ESP Affair.* Her novels and short stories have been translated into Japanese, Dutch, German, Italian, Norwegian, Spanish and Greek. When not writing sultry short stories, she edits erotic anthologies, including *Alison's Wonderland, Kiss My Ass, Skirting the Issue* and *Torn.* She is also the author of several novellas including *Cuffing Kate, Giving In* and *A Taste of Chi.*

Ms. Tyler is loyal to coffee (black), lipstick (red) and tequila (straight). She has tattoos, but no piercings; a wicked tongue, but a quick smile; and bittersweet memories, but no regrets. She believes it won't rain if she doesn't bring an umbrella, prefers hot and dry to cold and wet, and loves to spout her favorite motto: You can sleep when you're dead. She chooses Led Zeppelin over the Beatles, the Cure over NIN and the Stones over everyone. Yet although she appreciates good rock, she has a pitiful weakness for '80s hair bands.

In all things important, she remains faithful to her partner of eighteen years, but she still can't choose just one perfume.

PREVIOUSLY PUBLISHED STORIES EXCERPTED
IN THIS VOLUME ORIGINALLY APPEARED IN
THE FOLLOWING:

"Blue Denim Pussy," by Clarice Alexander, originally appeared in *Naughty Stories from A to Z* (Pretty Things Press). "Meltdown," by Jax Baynard, originally appeared in *The Big Book of Bondage* (Cleis Press). "A Story About Sarah," by Cheyenne Blue, originally appeared in *Lesbian Lust* (Cleis Press). Andrea Dale's "Now You See Her," originally appeared in *Peep Show* (Cleis Press); "Mrs. Claus and the Naughty Elf," originally appeared in *The MILF Anthology* (Blue Moon Books); "His Lady's Manservant," originally appeared in *Yes, Ma'am* (Cleis Press); "Paying It Forward," originally appeared in *Orgasmic* (Cleis Press); "Working Late," appeared in *She's on Top* (Cleis Press); "A Sensitive Sole" originally appeared in *The Sexiest Soles* (Alyson Books). "Nobody's Business," by Dante Davidson, originally appeared in *Sweet Life* (Cleis). "Quiet, Quiet," by Lucia Dixon, originally appeared in *Naughty Stories from A to Z* (Pretty Things Press). "Underground Encounter," by Tamsin Flowers, appeared in *Smut in the City* (House of Erotica). "Tripartite," by Georgia E. Jones, appeared in *Sudden Sex* (Cleis Press). *Make Mine to Go* by Dilo Keith (Breathless Press). "Spring Cleaning," by Samantha Mallery, originally appeared in *Naughty Stories from A to Z* (Pretty Things Press). "Smokehouse," by Sommer Marsden, originally appeared in *Smart Ass* (Pretty Things Press). "Pinch the Head," by Julia Moore, originally appeared in *Naughty Stories from A to Z* (Pretty Things Press). "Date Night," by N. T. Morley, originally appeared in *Morning, Noon and Night* (Cleis Press). "Underwater," by Emilie Paris, originally appeared in *Naughty Stories from A to Z* (Pretty Things Press). Giselle Renarde's "Clingy" originally appeared in *Erotic Tidbits* (Dallas Black); "Lillian's New

Toy" was originally published online at For The Girls; "Max Alone In See-Through Panties," was originally published online at Every Night Erotica; "The Couple with the Dragon Tattoo," originally appeared in *Partner Swap* (Xcite). "The Blindfold," by Donna George Storey, originally appeared in *Rain Crow*. Alison Tyler's "No Good Deed," originally appeared in *Please, Sir* (Cleis Press); "Boilermaker" originally appeared online on Fishnet (the blog for Blowfish); "Reunion" originally appeared in *Coupling 2* (Excessica); "Want" originally appeared in *Skirting the Issue* (Pretty Things Press); "Pierced" originally appeared on Bastardlife.com; "Wrapping It Up in Public" originally appeared in *Bondage on a Budget* (Masquerade Books); "Performance Anxiety" appeared in *Coupling 2* (Xcessica); *The Trade* was published by Pretty Things Press; "Seeing Stars" originally appeared in *One Night Only* (Cleis); "Zachary's Bed" originally appeared in *Bondage on a Budget* (Masquerade Books); "Last Call" originally appeared in *Morning, Noon and Night* (Cleis); "Burned" originally appeared in *The Big Book of Bondage Erotica* (Cleis); *Blue Valentine* was originally published by Magic Carpet Books; *Banging Rebecca* was originally published by Pretty Things Press; "Your Beautiful Launderette" originally appeared in *Bondage on a Budget* (Masquerade Books); "Playing for Keeps" originally appeared in *Bondage on a Budget* (Masquerade Books); "Obsessed" was published by Pretty Things Press; "The Last Goodbye" originally appeared in *Got a Minute?* (Cleis Press); "The Girl of His Dreams" originally appeared in *Bondage on a Budget* (Masquerade Books); "A Quick Ten" originally appeared *in Bondage on a Budget* (Masquerade Books); "Connecting" originally appeared in *Coupling 2* (Excessica); "Antonia's Beast" originally appeared in *Bondage on a Budget* (Masquerade); "Pegged" originally appeared in *Bad Ass* (Pretty Things Press); "Plucked" originally appeared in *Smart Ass* (Pretty Things Press); "Whose Panties" originally appeared in *Bondage on a Budget* (Masquerade Books); "Sailor Boy" originally appeared in *Bondage on a Budget* (Masquerade Books); "Like a Girl" originally appeared in *Crossdressing* (Cleis); "Broken" originally appeared in *Twisted* (Cleis Press); "Flash" originally appeared in *Bondage on a Budget* (Masquerade Books); "Not for Sale" originally appeared in *Stocking Up* (Pretty Things Press); "Rubbernecking" originally appeared in *Rubber Sex* (Cleis Press); "Mercury in Retrograde" originally appeared in *Open* (Pretty Things Press); "Counterpane" originally appeared on Bastardlife; "Four on the Floor" originally appeared in *Best Women's Erotica 2006* (Cleis Press). "The Trick in the Mirror," by Sharon Wachsler, originally appeared as "Tagged" in *Naughty or Nice: Christmas Erotica* (Cleis Press). Xan West's "Strong" originally appeared in *Say Please* (Cleis Press); "Nervous Boy" originally appeared in *Love at First Sting* (Cleis Press); "Compersion" originally appeared in *I Like to Watch* (Cleis Press). "Roger's Fault," by Eric Williams, originally appeared in *Naughty Stories from A to Z* (Pretty Things Press).

More from Alison Tyler

Frenzy
60 Stories of Sudden Sex
Edited by Alison Tyler

"Toss out the roses and box of candies. This isn't a prolonged seduction. This is slammed against the wall in an alleyway sex, and it's all that much hotter for it."
—Erotica Readers & Writers Association
ISBN 978-1-57344-331-9 $14.95

Best Bondage Erotica
Edited by Alison Tyler

Always playful and dangerously explicit, these arresting fantasies grab you, tie you down, and never let you go.
ISBN 978-1-57344-173-5 $15.95

Afternoon Delight
Erotica for Couples
Edited by Alison Tyler

"Alison Tyler evokes a world of heady sensuality where fantasies are fearlessly explored and dreams gloriously realized."
—Barbara Pizio, Executive Editor,
Penthouse Variations
ISBN 978-1-57344-341-8 $14.95

Got a Minute?
60 Second Erotica
Edited by Alison Tyler

"Classy but very, very dirty, this is one of the few very truly indispensable filth anthologies around." —*UK Forum*
ISBN 978-1-57344-404-0 $14.95

Playing with Fire
Taboo Erotica
Edited by Alison Tyler

"Alison Tyler has managed to find the best stories from the best authors, and create a book of fantasies that—if you're lucky enough, or determined enough—just might come true." —Clean Sheets
ISBN 978-1-57344-348-7 $14.95

* Free book of equal or lesser value. Shipping and applicable sales tax extra.
Cleis Press • (800) 780-2279 • orders@cleispress.com
www.cleispress.com

Happy Endings Forever And Ever

Buy 4 books, Get 1 FREE*

Dark Secret Love
A Story of Submission
By Alison Tyler

Inspired by her own BDSM exploits and private diaries, Alison Tyler draws on twenty-five years of penning sultry stories to create a scorchingly hot work of fiction, a memoir-inspired novel with reality at its core. A modern-day *Story of O*, a *9 1/2 Weeks*-style journey fueled by lust, longing and the search for true love.
ISBN 978-1-57344-956-4 $16.95

High-Octane Heroes
Erotic Romance for Women
Edited by Delilah Devlin

One glance and your heart will melt—these chiseled, brave men will ignite your fantasies with their courage and charisma. Award-winning romance writer Delilah Devlin has gathered stories of hunky, red-blooded guys who enter danger zones in the name of duty, honor, country and even love.
ISBN 978-1-57344-969-4 $15.95

Duty and Desire
Military Erotic Romance
Edited by Kristina Wright

The only thing stronger than the call of duty is the call of desire. *Duty and Desire* enlists a team of hot-blooded men and women from every branch of the military who serve their country and follow their hearts.
ISBN 978-1-57344-823-9 $15.95

Smokin' Hot Firemen
Erotic Romance Stories for Women
Edited by Delilah Devlin

Delilah delivers tales of these courageous men breaking down doors to steal readers' hearts! *Smokin' Hot Firemen* imagines the romantic possibilities of being held against a massively muscled chest by a man whose mission is to save lives and serve *every* need.
ISBN 978-1-57344-934-2 $15.95

Only You
Erotic Romance for Women
Edited by Rachel Kramer Bussel

Only You is full of tenderness, raw passion, love, longing and the many emotions that kindle true romance. The couples in *Only You* test the boundaries of their love to make their relationships stronger.
ISBN 978-1-57344-909-0 $15.95

* Free book of equal or lesser value. Shipping and applicable sales tax extra.
Cleis Press • (800) 780-2279 • orders@cleispress.com
www.cleispress.com

Many More Than Fifty Shades of Erotica

Buy 4 books, Get 1 FREE*

Please, Sir
Erotic Stories of Female Submission
Edited by Rachel Kramer Bussel

If you liked *Fifty Shades of Grey,* you'll love the explosive stories of *Please, Sir.* These damsels delight in the pleasures of taking risks to be rewarded by the men who know their deepest desires. Find out why nothing is as hot as the power of the words "Please, Sir."
ISBN 978-1-57344-389-0 $14.95

Yes, Sir
Erotic Stories of Female Submission
Edited by Rachel Kramer Bussel

Bound, gagged or spanked—or controlled with just a glance—these lucky women experience the breathtaking thrills of sexual submission. *Yes, Sir* shows that pleasure is best when dispensed by a firm hand.
ISBN 978-1-57344-310-4 $15.95

He's on Top
Erotic Stories of Male Dominance and Female Submission
Edited by Rachel Kramer Bussel

As true tops, the bossy hunks in these stories understand that BDSM is about exulting in power that is freely yielded. These kinky stories celebrate women who know exactly what they want.
ISBN 978-1-57344-270-1 $14.95

Best Bondage Erotica 2013
Edited by Rachel Kramer Bussel

Let *Best Bondage Erotica 2013* be your kinky playbook to erotic restraint—from silk ties and rope to shiny cuffs, blindfolds and so much more. These stories of forbidden desire will captivate, shock and arouse you.
ISBN 978-1-57344-897-0 $15.95

Luscious
Stories of Anal Eroticism
Edited by Alison Tyler

Discover all the erotic possibilities that exist between the sheets and between the cheeks in this daring collection. "Alison Tyler is an author to rely on for steamy, sexy page turners! Try her!"—Powell's Books
ISBN 978-1-57344-760-7 $15.95

* Free book of equal or lesser value. Shipping and applicable sales tax extra.
Cleis Press • (800) 780-2279 • orders@cleispress.com
www.cleispress.com

Unleash Your Favorite Fantasies

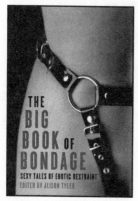

Buy 4 books, Get 1 FREE*

The Big Book of Bondage
Sexy Tales of Erotic Restraint
Edited by Alison Tyler

Nobody likes bondage more than editrix Alison Tyler, who is fascinated with the ecstasies of giving up, giving in, and entrusting one's pleasure (and pain) into the hands of another. Delve into a world of unrestrained passion, where heart-stopping dynamics will thrill and inspire you.
ISBN 978-1-57344-907-6 $15.95

Hurts So Good
Unrestrained Erotica
Edited by Alison Tyler
Intricately secured by ropes, locked in handcuffs or bound simply by a lover's command, the characters of *Hurts So Good* find themselves in the throes of pleasurable restraint in this indispensible collection by prolific, award-winning editor Alison Tyler.
ISBN 978-1-57344-723-2 $14.95

Caught Looking
Erotic Tales of Voyeurs and Exhibitionists
Edited by Alison Tyler
and Rachel Kramer Bussel

These scintillating fantasies take the reader inside a world where people get to show off, watch, and feel the vicarious thrill of sex times two, their erotic power multiplied by the eyes of another.
ISBN 978-1-57344-256-5 $14.95

Hide and Seek
Erotic Tales of Voyeurs and Exhibitionists
Edited by Rachel Kramer Bussel
and Alison Tyler

Whether putting on a deliberate show for an eager audience or peeking into the hidden sex lives of their neighbors, these show-offs and shy types go all out in their quest for the perfect peep show.
ISBN 978-1-57344-419-4 $14.95

One Night Only
Erotic Encounters
Edited by Violet Blue

"Passion and lust play by different rules in *One Night Only*. These are stories about what happens when we have just that one opportunity to ask for what we want—and we take it… Enjoy the adventure."
—Violet Blue
ISBN 978-1-57344-756-0 $14.95

* Free book of equal or lesser value. Shipping and applicable sales tax extra.
Cleis Press • (800) 780-2279 • orders@cleispress.com
www.cleispress.com

Bestselling Erotica for Couples

Buy 4 books,
Get 1 *FREE**

Sweet Life
Erotic Fantasies for Couples
Edited by Violet Blue

Your ticket to a front row seat for first-time spankings,
breathtaking role-playing scenes, sex parties, women who
strap it on and men who love to take it, not to mention
threesomes of every combination.
ISBN 978-1-57344-133-9 $14.95

Sweet Life 2
Erotic Fantasies for Couples
Edited by Violet Blue

"This is a we-did-it-you-can-too anthology of real couples playing out their fantasies." —Lou Paget, author of *365 Days of
Sensational Sex*
ISBN 978-1-57344-167-4 $15.95

Sweet Love
Erotic Fantasies for Couples
Edited by Violet Blue

"If you ever get a chance to try out your
number-one fantasies in real life—and I as-
sure you, there will be more than one—say
yes. It's well worth it. May this book, its
adventurous authors, and the daring and
satisfied characters be your guiding inspira-
tion."—Violet Blue
ISBN 978-1-57344-381-4 $14.95

Afternoon Delight
Erotica for Couples
Edited by Alison Tyler

"Alison Tyler evokes a world of heady sensuality where fantasies are fearlessly explored and dreams gloriously realized."
—Barbara Pizio, Executive Editor, *Penthouse Variations*
ISBN 978-1-57344-341-8 $14.95

Three-Way
Erotic Stories
Edited by Alison Tyler

"Three means more of everything. Maybe
I'm greedy, but when it comes to sex, I like
more. More fingers. More tongues. More
limbs. More tangling and wrestling on the
mattress."
ISBN 978-1-57344-193-3 $15.95

* Free book of equal or lesser value. Shipping and applicable sales tax extra.
Cleis Press • (800) 780-2279 • orders@cleispress.com
www.cleispress.com

THE ULTIMATE GUIDES

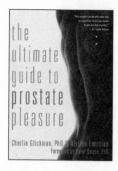

"Vanillas, novices, old hands, old guard—everyone can learn from this collection."

—Dan Savage

The Ultimate Guide to Prostate Pleasure
Erotic Exploration for Men and Their Partners

Charlie Glickman, PhD and Aislinn Emirzian

$17.95, 6" x 9", 368 Pages,
Health/Sexuality,
ISBN: 978-1-57344-904-5,
Trade Paper, 32/case,
Rights: World

The Ultimate Guide to Kink
BDSM, Role Play and the Erotic Edge

Tristan Taormino

$19.95, 6" x 9", 464 Pages,
Sexuality,
ISBN: 978-1-57344-779-9,
Trade Paper, 28/case,
Rights: World

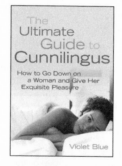

The Ultimate Guide to Orgasm for Women
How to Become Orgasmic for a Lifetime

Mikaya Heart

$17.95, 6" x 9", 272 Pages,
Health/Sexuality,
ISBN: 978-1-57344-711-9,
Trade Paper, 40/case,
Rights: World

The Ultimate Guide to Cunnilingus
How to Go Down on a Woman and Give Her Exquisite Pleasure

Violet Blue

$16.95, 6" x 9", 200 Pages,
Sexuality,
ISBN: 978-1-57344-387-6,
Trade Paper, 52/case,
Rights: World

The Ultimate Guide to Fellatio
How to Go Down on a Man and Give Him Mind-Blowing Pleasure

Violet Blue

$16.95, 6" x 9", 272 Pages,
Sexuality,
ISBN: 978-1-57344-398-2,
Trade Paper, 36/case,
Rights: World

THE ULTIMATE GUIDES

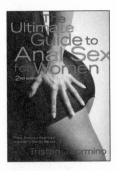

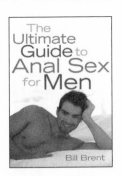

The Ultimate Guide to Anal Sex for Women

Tristan Taormino

$16.95, 6" x 9", 240 Pages,
Sexuality,
ISBN: 978-1-57344-221-3,
Trade Paper, 40/case,
Rights: World

The Ultimate Guide to Pregnancy for Lesbians
How to Stay Sane and Care for Yourself from Pre-conception Through Birth

Rachel Pepper

$17.95, 6" x 9", 288 Pages,
Health/Pregnancy & Childbirth,
ISBN: 978-1-57344-216-9,
Trade Paper, 36/case,
Rights: World

The Ultimate Guide to Anal Sex for Men

Bill Brent

$16.95, 6" x 9", 272 Pages,
Sexuality,
ISBN: 978-1-57344-121-6,
Trade Paper, 36/case,
Rights: World

The Ultimate Guide to Sexual Fantasy
How to Turn Your Fantasies into Reality

Violet Blue

$15.95, 6" x 9", 272 Pages,
Sexuality,
ISBN: 978-1-57344-190-2,
Trade Paper, 32/case,
Rights: World

The Ultimate Guide to Sex and Disability
For All of Us Who Live with Disabilities, Chronic Pain and Illness

Miriam Kaufman, M.D., Cory Silverberg and Fran Odette

$18.95, 6" x 9", 360 Pages,
Health/Sexuality,
ISBN: 978-1-57344-304-3,
Trade Paper, 24/case,
Rights: World

"A welcome resource.... This book will be a worthwhile read for anyone who lives with a disability, loves someone with a disability, or simply wants to be better informed sexually."
—Curve

Classic Sex Guides

Buy 4 books,
Get 1 FREE*

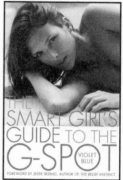

The Smart Girl's Guide to the G-Spot
Violet Blue

It's not a myth, it's a miracle, the G-spot, that powerhouse of female orgasm. With wit and panache, sex educator and bestselling writer Violet Blue helps readers master the sexual alphabet through G.
ISBN 978-1-57344-780-5 $14.95

The Smart Girl's Guide to Porn
Violet Blue

As seen on the Oprah Winfrey show!
Looking for authentic sex scenes? Thinking of sharing porn with a lover? Wonder which browser is safest for Internet porn surfing? *The Smart Girl's Guide to Porn* has the answers.
ISBN 978-1-57344-247-3 $14.95

The Adventurous Couple's Guide to Sex Toys
Violet Blue

Feeling adventurous? In this witty and well-informed consumer guide, bestselling author and sex educator Violet Blue shows couples how to choose and use sex toys to play and explore together—and have mind-blowing sex.
ISBN 978-1-57344-972-4 $14.95

The Adventurous Couple's Guide to Strap-On Sex
Violet Blue

"If you're seriously considering making it a part of your sexual repertoire, *The Adventurous Couple's Guide to Strap-On Sex* will give you all the advice you need to enjoy it in a safe and satisfying fashion" —*Forum UK*
ISBN 978-1-57344-278-7 $14.95

Seal It With a Kiss
Violet Blue

A great kiss can stop traffic, start a five-alarm fire, and feel like Times Square on New Year's Eve. Get your smooch on with all the different tricks and tips found in *Seal It with a Kiss*.
ISBN 978-1-57344-385-2 $12.95

---

* Free book of equal or lesser value. Shipping and applicable sales tax extra.
Cleis Press • (800) 780-2279 • orders@cleispress.com
www.cleispress.com

Ordering is easy! Call us toll free or fax us to place your MC/VISA order.
You can also mail the order form below with payment to:
Cleis Press, 2246 Sixth St., Berkeley, CA 94710.

ORDER FORM

QTY	TITLE	PRICE

SUBTOTAL _____

SHIPPING _____

SALES TAX _____

TOTAL _____

Add $3.95 postage/handling for the first book ordered and $1.00 for each additional book. Outside North America, please contact us for shipping rates. California residents add 9% sales tax. Payment in U.S. dollars only.

★ Free book of equal or lesser value. Shipping and applicable sales tax extra.

Cleis Press • Phone: (800) 780-2279 • Fax: (510) 845-8001
orders@cleispress.com • www.cleispress.com
You'll find more great books on our website

Follow us on Twitter @cleispress • Friend/fan us on Facebook